TWO
CHINESE
STATES

TWO
CHINESE
STATES

U.S. FOREIGN POLICY AND INTERESTS

EDITED BY RAMON H. MYERS

INTRODUCTION BY ROBERT A. SCALAPINO

HOOVER INSTITUTION PRESS
Stanford University, Stanford, California

Hoover Institution Publication 200

TYPESET BY TED LIGDA, REDWOOD CITY, CALIFORNIA

contents

foreword

The inability of the United States to help non-communist governments in Southeast Asia defeat communist insurgency during the 1970s has raised serious questions concerning the limits of American power and how such power should be used to serve the national interest throughout the world.

Nowhere are these questions more important today than in East Asia. Since former President Richard M. Nixon's historic visit to the People's Republic of China, the United States has come to recognize that there is only one China. It is well-known, however, that two governments exist. Each claims to represent China: the Republic of China (ROC) on Taiwan plus the Pescadore Islands and the People's Republic of China (PRC) on the Asian mainland.

How should the United States deal with these political entities, as isolationist sentiment grows at home?

This book offers a new East Asian policy for the United States, particularly toward regimes that claim to represent China. It should be made clear, as this study attempts to do, that this proposal does not advance a "two-China policy." Rather, it represents a foreign policy that can be applied to any part of the world today and adapted to regions where American power remains limited.

This proposed policy stresses the need for the United States to maintain a balance of power between all of the individual and individualistic nations of East Asia as well as between other countries which have vested interests in that area of the world. This is essential in order to preserve the fragile stability and security of the region. It is suggested that the United States use it negotiating skill and influence to establish bilateral agreements that maintain and strengthen, rather than weaken, existing arrangements among countries in East Asia.

As for the two political regimes, the ROC and the PRC, the new policy

would comprise an American diplomatic strategy for developing numerous bilateral agreements with both governments for the purpose of maintaining a series of international alignments: the USSR and Japan, the USSR and the PRC, North Korea and South Korea, the PRC and the ROC. Such an American strategy should ultimately lead to normal diplomatic relations between the United States and the PRC, which almost exist today, while the United States continues to maintain and strengthen its military, political, legal, and economic relations with the ROC.

The editor of this monograph, Ramon H. Myers, has attracted a distinguished group of scholars to argue the advantages of such a proposed policy for the United States throughout East Asia. It is a pleasure to add this book as the fourth volume in the Hoover Institution's new International Studies series on current problems and issues that are critically important to American national interests.

RICHARD F. STAAR
Coordinator of International Studies
Hoover Institution

Stanford, California

preface

In the Shanghai Communiqué of February 1972, the United States declared its agreement with the contention that "all Chinese on either side of the Taiwan Strait maintain there is but one China and that Taiwan is a part of China." Thus the United States gave birth to a new China. Trade and exchanges of people between the United States and the People's Republic of China (PRC) rapidly increased. As a result, many experts began urging the United States to establish full diplomatic relations with the PRC as soon as possible.

The leaders of the PRC, however, set a high price on the establishment of normal relations between the two countries. They insisted that the United States make three major concessions: (1) the abrogation of the 1954 Mutual Security Treaty with the Republic of China (ROC) on Taiwan; (2) the removal of all U.S. military forces from the ROC; and (3) the severing of diplomatic ties with the ROC.

If Washington agrees to pay Peking's price for normalization of relations, is a new era of cooperation in East Asia either possible or likely? If not, what policy should the United States adopt toward China to reduce the possibility of conflict in East Asia? The purpose of this study is to chart a policy for the United States in its future relationships with the two regimes, the Republic of China and the People's Republic of China, that will be in its own best interest.

Dr. Robert Scalapino's introduction advances three alternative foreign-policy strategies in East Asia bearing on the China problem. These strategies can be neither reconciled nor combined: they are mutually exclusive. Each presents certain advantages and disadvantages for the United States.

The four essays that follow argue in favor of the "equilibrium strategy" cited in the introduction. This strategy requires the United States to use its

diplomatic skills to preserve a stable balance of power among the regimes in East Asia. Throughout history, nation-states have achieved maximum economic development and social progress only when power has been evenly distributed among them through sufficient checks and balances. When the system of checks and balances has become inadequate or has broken down, creating an uneven distribution of power among states, conflict has become inevitable. War rather than peace has prevailed; economic and social retrogression has become the norm.

The full range of American economic, cultural, and scientific interests in East Asia can be realized only if a balance of power is maintained, but this can occur only if each new issue or problem is negotiated individually with prudence and patience, and if reckless actions that might upset any of the relationships are avoided. Package-agreement diplomacy (a complex series of agreements that are closely interrelated and likely to have broad implications for long-term relationships between states) should be shunned. Such agreements between two states involve great uncertainty and risk that can prove dangerous for global stability. Other states can perceive these new arrangements as threats to their interests in ways the negotiating parties view as unimportant. Such agreements can also reduce the ability of either negotiating party to act according to its best interests on other issues or elsewhere in the globe. Therefore, cautious, gradual negotiation of single issues on a step-by-step basis—the diplomatic style of the "equilibrium strategy"—seems a better approach.

William W. Whitson's essay outlines the two principal views of the way American power has been used in the world since 1945 to advance the best interests of the United States. Each of these two viewpoints yields a different strategy for the establishment of normal diplomatic relations between the United States and the PRC; and either strategy—meeting Peking's current conditions or resorting to the negotiating tactics inherent in the "equilibrium strategy" to achieve normalization more gradually—will have profound implications for American interests in East Asia.

The United States has had economic relations with both the PRC and the ROC for the past six years; the benefits of the connections for the United States are outlined in the essay by Norma Schroder. She argues that trade between the United States and the PRC can continue to expand if various bilateral agreements can be concluded. On the other hand, she notes that a precipitous break between the United States and the ROC carries a high risk of great economic losses for the United States in particular and for East Asia in general. Therefore, if the United States can achieve normal relations with

the PRC through the negotiating tactics inherent in the "equilibrium strategy," economic ties between the United States and the two China regimes will continue to prosper, to the benefit of all parties.

The essay by C. Martin Wilbur illuminates the dramatic modernization that is already taking place in the ROC and shows that it can be expected to continue as long as the government on Taiwan can be guaranteed its sovereignty and military security. Wilbur's candid description of the economic achievements of the ROC, the gradual stirrings of grass-roots democracy there, and the continuing problem of a repressive government provides a refreshing counterweight to the singularly flattering image of the PRC that most visitors have conveyed in their reports. Travellers to the PRC simply cannot go behind the scenes to learn about the "dark shadows" of that society as a critical observer like Wilbur can do in the ROC. He reminds us that a society like the ROC that permits some freedom to both citizens and visitors deserves support and encouragement so that it can become even more open.

Each of the China regimes has achieved legitimacy in governing its respective geographical territory. The long-standing differences between them will eventually be resolved only by the Chinese people, but the resolution is more likely to be peaceful if a stable balance of power can be maintained among all of the states in East Asia. In the final essay, I argue that American interests in East Asia are best served by a strategy that commits the United States to a "balancer" role there.

The first requirement of the "equilibrium strategy" as a means of promoting normal relations between Washington and Peking is a moratorium on all future consideration of "package agreements." The second is agreement by both sides upon an agenda of separately negotiable issues that can gradually be resolved in a series of bilateral agreements, broadening exchanges of all kinds. Such a gradualist approach requires not only great negotiating skills, but also considerable perseverance and enormous patience—qualities that have rarely characterized American diplomats in the past. This is partly because the United States has previously lacked a clearly articulated strategy aimed at preserving a stable power balance around the world, and partly because of the eagerness of our negotiators to report quick results. By dealing with only one issue at a time, the United States can maintain its flexibility in other areas of negotiation. This approach can dispel the current frustration on both sides over the failure to normalize relations between Washington and Peking and pave the way for future cooperation rather than conflict in East Asia.

The recommendations of this policy study will not satisfy fervent isolationists who believe that the United States should reduce its influence and respon-

sibilities in the world. Nor will it satisfy those who adhere to the "grand-design" school of foreign policy, which maintains that only the major world powers can achieve workable arrangements for resolving global conflicts and achieving international cooperation. While the "equilibrium strategy" as a basis for diplomacy will find little support from either extreme of current opinion, it does translate popular sentiment at home into a viable China policy for the United States.

A poll taken in August 1977 of eighteen hundred individuals connected with various branches of government and the public media found that although a majority wanted "normal" relations with the PRC, an even larger majority insisted that the United States maintain its present relations with the ROC.[1] In other words, the majority of those who represent the American people and interpret current events for them want their country to have the same diplomatic ties with each of the two regimes that claim to represent China. A new approach that enables the United States to pursue its interests and maintain its commitments in East Asia while translating popular sentiment into a workable China policy certainly deserves careful consideration.

---

[1] Michael Y. M. Kau, Pierre M. Perrolle, Susan H. Marsh, and Jeffrey Berman, "Public Opinion and Our China Policy," *Asian Affairs* 5, no. 3 (January–February 1978): 133–47.

acknowledgments

The editor wishes to express his thanks to Professor Richard Walker of the University of South Carolina, Dr. Fu-mei Chen Chang of the Hoover Institution, and Professor Thomas Metzger of the University of California at San Diego for critical comments on this manuscript in early drafts. Their suggestions for improvement in the final manuscript greatly helped the editor in his task. Dr. Ming Chan, a former national fellow of the Hoover Institution, and Molly Sturges of the Hoover Institution also provided useful editorial suggestions. None of the above are responsible for errors or infelicities of expression that may remain.

RAMON MYERS
Hoover Institution

robert a.   introduction
scalapino

In 1978 American foreign policy remains unclear and, for the most part, unpredictable. There are, to be sure, some important issues upon which the United States has spoken officially with seeming clarity; most of these pertain to Europe. In these statements the Carter administration has essentially reiterated the policies of the past: a commitment to NATO and the defense of Western Europe against external aggression; moral support, coupled with some political-economic encouragement, to governments within the liberal democratic spectrum and to those East European states considered most promising as independent political entities; and assurances of continued concern over the international economic order, especially the nature of relations among advanced industrial nations.

Like most administrations in American history, the Carter administration is strongly Europocentric; within this context, it tends to focus heavily upon its competitive position vis-à-vis the Soviet Union.

Even with respect to Europe, however, many specific issues and, more important, many questions of basic strategy remain unresolved. What are the respective obligations of the United States and its European allies in the security realm, and what basic strategy should govern security policies for Europe? What are the principles that should apply to détente with the USSR and other states that are based upon radically different political-economic

systems: can and should reciprocity and accountability be demanded, or can we profit from unilateralism on occasion? What is the appropriate relation between a commitment to human rights and a commitment to security, both ours and that of others? And what are the yardsticks to be used in defining and grading human rights? This is but a small sample of the unresolved or unclarified issues, some of which are crucial in the ultimate shaping of U.S. foreign policy.

It has been argued that at present, given the fluidity of international politics and the impossibility of resolving certain problems, a lack of clarity in American foreign policy may be not only a necessity, but even an asset. Keeping one's options open while awaiting further developments has its merits, particularly if it is difficult to know what the political and economic situations are going to be. The problems engendered by such an approach, however, especially when applied on the current scale, should be obvious. The United States remains the most powerful single nation in the world, all aspects of power considered. Its actions or failures to act, the coherence or lack of coherence that marks its policies, and its leadership or lack of leadership in such critical fields as international monetary policy all do much to shape our times. The abdication of authority is as meaningful a policy as the willingness to pursue initiatives.

In Asia, the current scene is particularly fluid. In effect, three different strategies are competing for support, with the contest still unresolved. One may be labelled the withdrawal strategy. In essence, it calls for the withdrawal of the United States from Asia and from much of the Western Pacific, with commitments of American military forces restricted to America's territories in the Pacific. This strategy would not preclude economic and political interaction with Asian states, but it would effectively end the era of defense treaties and the American commitment to direct military support to maintain a strategic equilibrium in Asia.

A second possibility is the united-front strategy. Essentially, it rests upon a simple thesis: since the Soviet Union is the only power that can threaten the United States physically, and since Soviet military strength continues to grow in Asia as elsewhere, accompanied by policies that challenge the interests of many states of the region, the United States should align itself with all states that are prepared to resist the USSR. This would include nations of diverse political and socioeconomic structures. Thus, the adherents of this strategy would view a U.S.–Japan–People's Republic of China combination as a logical one.

A third alternative might be labelled the equilibrium strategy. It is based

upon several key propositions. First, in relations with the two communist giants, the interests of the United States are best served by avoiding an alliance or a sustained "tilt" toward either nation. Rather, the United States should adopt a policy of issue-by-issue negotiation, with our interests and those of our allies determining our position, and with the principles of reciprocity and accountability made requirements of important agreements. Second, the United States should retain certain strategic commitments in the Pacific-Asian region, both because such commitments remain necessary if a broader strategic equilibrium is to survive and because the principle of negotiating from strength must at this stage include military as well as other forms of power.

Granted that none of these strategies need be, or is likely to be, applied in its pure form, it is my view that the equilibrium strategy is the only one that will serve our interests and those of the Asian states with which we are most closely associated. An alliance with China against Russia, for example, even a de-facto alignment, would not only evoke multiple Soviet countermeasures rendering agreements between the United States and the USSR difficult if not impossible to reach; it would also destabilize the Pacific-Asian region by significantly advancing the power of the People's Republic of China, a nation that is not only communist but also strongly nationalist in character—and by no means satisfied with the Asian status quo. In any case, until basic strategic decisions are made, our Asian policies will continue to be improvisations, with limited integration or certainty of tenure.

Meanwhile, both as a nation and as concerned individuals, we wrestle with "the China problem," with no easy resolution in sight. China-Taiwan fits broadly into the category we have labelled "divided states," a legacy of World War II and its immediate aftermath. What has happened to the other "divided states" to date? The German issue has been settled peacefully, at least for this era. The problem of Vietnam was resolved by force. Korea remains a thorny and potentially dangerous problem, as does China. In none of these cases has peaceful unification been achieved.

In each of these situations international involvement has been extensive; this is understandable. Without exception, the initial divisions were products of international developments and commitments, not purely indigenous events, and international commitments are still shaping to a very considerable extent current trends: they will probably determine the ultimate outcomes. The knowledge that the USSR would not countenance a unified, noncommunist Germany, for example, certainly influenced the German "solution." The American commitment to South Korea—uncertain until it was tested in 1950— was critical to the survival of the Republic of Korea. Conversely, the U.S.

abandonment of the Republic of Vietnam was decisive in the fate of the non-communist Vietnamese.

Every situation, to be sure, is *sui generis* in some respects, and that is clearly the case with the China-Taiwan issue. In population and size, the disparity between "the two Chinas" is enormous. The People's Republic of China has a population estimated at between 850 million and more than 950 million (the latter figure is the one used by most U.S. government specialists), compared with approximately 17 million people on Taiwan. The disparity in land area is even greater. When the economic statistics are considered, however, Taiwan has the advantage in some areas, as Norma Schroder's essay indicates. Taiwan's annual rate of growth and its per-capita income made it one of the more prosperous societies of East Asia, second only to Japan in that region. In contrast, the economic performance of the PRC, while satisfactory, is in no sense spectacular, and the substantial problems that remain to be faced have been frankly admitted by Peking leaders. In sum, the disparity in standards of living is extraordinarily great. Taiwan is one of the few affluent societies of the world; the People's Republic of China is one of the poorer nations. To be sure, this is not merely because of the relative merits of their different economic systems or strategies it also involves the critical issue of scale. The modernization of a country with a population of nearly one billion, even under optimal conditions and with no policy errors, constitutes a prodigious task—one that cannot be consummated quickly.

Understandably, few individuals living in Taiwan would voluntarily opt for amalgamation with the PRC, not merely for economic reasons, but also because of the sizable disparities between these two societies in values, life-style, and sociopolitical conditions. Despite various pronouncements to the contrary, there is not "one China" at present, nor is there likely to be in the foreseeable future—barring the use of force. We and the world are confronted with two de-facto states, both viable and growing apart rather than together with the passage of time. There are, of course, other Chinas in Asia as well—Hong Kong and Singapore, each with its unique characteristics and special circumstances, but these are much less significant in world politics.

Given these facts, it is natural that the prevailing sentiment among the American citizenry, political leadership, and academic-journalistic community can be succinctly summarized in the acronym HOC BEIT, "Having One's Cake, But Eating It Too." The desire to "normalize" relations with the PRC, an objective of the Carter administration, is broadly shared. The term "normalization" is an unfortunate one, since it is doubtful that any nation has truly "normal" relations with the PRC and since the United States clearly has closer

relations with Peking in certain respects than many states with ambassadors in that capital. However, "normalization" of relations has become a synonym for the establishment of full diplomatic relations, and as a general principle, the legal recognition of all de-facto states has considerable merit—provided that the price for such a policy is not too high. But is not the Republic of China on Taiwan also a de-facto state? No one can realistically argue that Taiwan is a part of China today, nor that it has been in recent decades. Moreover, a considerable majority of both the American people and the American elite are opposed to abrogating all political and military ties with Taiwan as the price for recognition of the PRC. They favor continuing U.S. ties with Taiwan while expanding those with the PRC. Even the strong proponents of rapid diplomatic recognition of the PRC are quick to deny that they want the United States to abandon Taiwan; indeed, there is an element of humor in the lengths to which most such individuals will go to defend themselves against the latter charge. Those who advocate the most extreme policy—fully accepting Peking's conditions for "normalization" of relations and cutting the Republic of China on Taiwan totally adrift politically and militarily—insist that this will make Taiwan more self-reliant and stronger, and that it will provide the ROC with added incentive for reasonable negotiations with the PRC, out of which will come happiness and contentment for all.

Few observers, to be sure, have this simple faith. It is widely recognized that the security issue is the critical one; hence, various formulas have been advanced by those advocating rapid normalization. Generally, they hinge upon a unilateral declaration by the United States, via either the president or the Congress, at the time when formal diplomatic recognition of the PRC occurs, that the United States is committed to the peaceful settlement of the Taiwan issue, and that until such a settlement is achieved, it will continue to make military equipment available to Taiwan for the ROC's defense.

Proponents of this approach defend it by contending that although the United States can never obtain from the PRC a formal agreement on the non-use of force, it may be able to extract from Peking a silence—to be interpreted as acquiescence—in response to such a unilateral declaration by the United States. Unfortunately for the proponents of this approach, PRC spokesmen have chosen not to be silent in the recent past. On the contrary, they have spoken volubly, asserting that not only will the PRC not accept the "nonuse of force" principle, it also will not tolerate any unilateral American declaration on the Taiwan question, or the shipment of military supplies to Taiwan in a postnormalization period.

Apart from these stark facts, the fatal weakness in the formula outlined

above is that with full recognition of the PRC and derecognition of Taiwan, the United States—either de jure or de facto—will have accepted the position that Taiwan is a part of China. How then can the United States—without the specific approval of the sovereign state involved—furnish arms to Taiwan or in any other manner conduct separate policies toward it without being accused both at home and abroad of interference in the internal affairs of another state?

In truth, at present no formula that is acceptable to the People's Republic of China also provides the degree of security to the Republic of China on Taiwan that is necessary to any peaceful resolution of the issue. The most appealing formula to many, because it accords both with current reality and with historical American moral principles, is the so-called German approach—namely, that the people on Taiwan, having long enjoyed independence, should not be coerced into becoming a province of a nation to which they do not wish to be attached. Thus, adherents of this theory argue, a recognition of the two states more or less in terms of the peoples over whom they have actual jurisdiction is the soundest policy, accompanied by a willingness to wait until both or either is prepared to accept formal recognition on such terms. The response from opponents is that since the PRC would never accept this formula, it moves away from, rather than toward, solution of the problem.

Another formula would require that explicit agreement, not merely a "tacit" or "under-the-table" understanding, between the United States and the PRC would have to be reached on the questions of nonuse of force and Taiwan's right of access to defense materials prior to full-fledged diplomatic recognition of the PRC. The proponents of this position assert that a unilateral American declaration or a tacit agreement, even if either was acceptable to a given group of Peking's leaders, would be certain to cause future trouble between Washington and Peking. Either solution would ensure that Taiwan would become an acrimonious issue at some point, since domestic political considerations would require a disavowal by Peking's leadership—present or future—that any "secret deal" had been made or "informal understanding" reached with respect to Taiwan. Just as the Chinese and American interpretations of the ambiguous Shanghai Communiqué now differ, so the issue of Taiwan would present a much graver point of contention. Rather than providing for closer relations, therefore, normalization of relations between the United States and the PRC via tacit agreement might well lead to a deterioration of relations, and this might occur in a context where the bulk of the legal arguments would clearly lie on the side of the PRC.

The proponents of maximal concessions to the PRC make the same response to the insistence upon explicit agreements regarding the nonuse of force and

Taiwan's right of access to defense materials pending a peaceful settlement that they make to the "German solution": it is not acceptable to Peking. As we have noted, however, *nothing* is currently acceptable to the PRC short of its own position, namely, the breaking of diplomatic relations with the Republic of China on Taiwan, the removal of all American forces and installations from Taiwan, and the abrogation of the Mutual Security Treaty—in sum, the restriction of ties between the United States and Taiwan to purely economic ones, subject to the approval of the PRC. In fact, Peking has rejected *all* American formulas to date. This attitude could change, but in the meantime, in this era when the U.S. government is heralding its championship of human rights, is it inappropriate to ask whether this policy extends to the human rights of the people on Taiwan? If the People's Republic of China has principles, should not the United States also proclaim the fact that it has its own?

Why—given the risks to American credibility and the basic moral questions involved—do a number of able individuals, not ideologues but in many cases longtime students of China, advocate the course of maximal concessions? One undeniable factor in many cases is Sinophilia—that magnetic pull China has upon its students and devotees; its attraction may be paralleled only by the hold India has had on some of its American adherents. The powerful attraction of Chinese culture, the extraordinary appeal of the Chinese people, and the unforgettable memories of Chinese hospitality cut across political barriers.

Apart from emotional attachments, however, four central reasons are advanced for effecting a change in our relations with the People's Republic of China now:

1. If the United States does not normalize its relations with the People's Republic of China, and resolve, or at least finesse, the Taiwan issue quickly, the possibility or even probability that a discouraged, disillusioned PRC will turn back toward the Soviet Union will steadily grow. Once again, the United States may be confronted with a Sino-Soviet alliance.

2. To allow the Taiwan issue to continue unresolved risks a confrontation in ten to fifteen years, when China will have the military power as well as the desire to "liberate" the island.

3. If such "liberation" should occur, the American people would strongly resist military involvement with China on behalf of Taiwan, and the U.S. government would face the painful dilemma of either plunging into an unpopular war or reneging on a firm commitment.

4. The chances of influencing the internal development of the People's Republic, including promoting the type of economic and technical development that will emphasize internal growth rather than external expansion, is greatest if our relations with the PRC are maximal rather than minimal.

There are no certainties in international politics, and each of these contentions deserves serious consideration because none can be regarded as wholly illogical. It may be remembered that prior to Mao's death, one of the arguments for rapid normalization of relations was that if it did not take place before he passed from the scene, a post-Mao leadership might well revert to détente with the USSR. Clearly, that has not happened. Sino-Soviet relations are still marked by the same degree of bitterness and hostility that has prevailed since the 1960s.

The restoration of the type of ties that produced the Sino-Soviet alliance, however, seems far less likely. It is not merely that historic cultural and ethnic rivalries persist, revitalized by the bitter struggles of the past two decades; of at least equal importance is the fact that two great continental empires are now moving toward each other, seeking to populate and develop their mutual borders with no buffer-state system to separate them. The potential for political and military rivalry is heightened, moreover, by the presence of large groups of minority peoples on both sides of the lengthy Chinese-Russian border, peoples who generally regard themselves as victims of discrimination.

It thus seems unlikely that a renewed Sino-Soviet alliance lies ahead, but full-fledged war also seems improbable, since neither party could conceivably benefit from such a conflict. Of immediate importance to our considerations, however, is a separate issue: is the Taiwan problem the critical variable in determining the timing and degree of Sino-Soviet accommodation? Analysis of the massive flow of statements, editorials, and official party pronouncements coming out of the People's Republic of China shows that the issue presently of the greatest concern to Peking's leaders is not Taiwan, but the uncertainty of America's credibility vis-à-vis that of the Soviet Union. China's present foreign policy essentially rests upon conventional balance-of-power principles. The role assigned the United States is that of counterweight to the USSR. Should Peking come to doubt seriously the will or capacity of the United States to play that role, it would have to reevaluate its basic foreign policies, and it might well be forced to seek at least a limited détente with Moscow. Chinese power alone is no match for Soviet power, nor will it be in the foreseeable future. Thus, of great significance for the future of Sino-Soviet relations is an

American variable; it is not our policy toward Taiwan but rather our general credibility as a global power.

I should add that this role does not require the United States to take up a wholly confrontational position toward the USSR, let alone play out the scenario repeatedly outlined by Peking: World War III, fought primarily in Europe and with the two nuclear giants eliminating each other, leaving the international stage to "true socialism." Nevertheless, it is important to keep in mind the fact that if the United States were to pursue the withdrawal strategy outlined earlier, or some close approximation of that strategy, the repercussions upon Chinese foreign policy would be substantial. Moreover, while the PRC would be overjoyed to see the United States abandon Taiwan, would not such an action inevitably create in its aftermath new doubts about American credibility throughout Asia, not merely in Tokyo, Seoul, and Singapore, but also in Peking?

The thesis that failure to resolve the Taiwan issue may ultimately lead to a Sino-American war has credibility only if it is assumed, first, that the PRC elects to attempt the "liberation" of Taiwan by force, and second, that the American commitment is sufficiently minimal or ambiguous to make the authorities in Peking feel that they are taking little risk. It must not be forgotten that the two Asian wars in which we have participated since 1945 were both largely the products of communist miscalculation—a fact that highlights the dangers of leaving American commitments unclear.

It is inconceivable that the PRC leaders would knowingly risk a war with the United States over Taiwan, now or in the foreseeable future. Our military strength will continue to be vastly greater than China's, with the gap probably widening rather than narrowing in the decades immediately ahead. Moreover, if the PRC's present plan of turning outward for advanced science and technology is carried out, the links between the PRC, Japan, and the developed Western nations including the United States will undoubtedly be much greater during the next ten to fifteen years. Finally, if Peking's leaders perceive a clear-cut American commitment to Taiwan, will they not also realize that such a war would produce extraordinarily high military costs as well as severe economic losses resulting from the disruption of their trade with Japan and Western Europe?

Indeed, this thesis contradicts another view generally put forth by those who want to cut political and military ties with Taiwan—that the PRC has no intention of using military force to "liberate" the island. For the immediate future, this second theory is almost certainly correct. In the longer run, however, *in the absence of any American security commitment*, the temptation to

use force is likely to become overpowering. It should be noted that there are many uses of force short of an actual invasion; among them is a naval-aerial blockade. At this point, the Taiwan issue is subdued in Chinese domestic politics because the American commitment makes any resort to force wholly unrealistic. If that commitment were removed, the pressure to take a more militant posture toward Taiwan would almost certainly grow during the next ten to fifteen years and a growing Chinese military capability would make such a posture credible against an isolated Taiwan. The real threat of war lies here.

The third thesis is in some respects the most telling, given the recent background of Vietnam, and the pendulum-like swing toward American retrenchment in the world, at least in Asia. The argument that the American people would not support a military conflict to defend Taiwan, and that therefore our current treaty commitments are not credible is, on the surface, an effective one. Korea and Vietnam raise the serious question whether the United States can ever again fight a protracted, limited war; certainly the prospect of sending large numbers of American men to any part of Asia seems remote at present. Indeed, this was the principal reason for the enunciation of the so-called Guam Doctrine during the Nixon administration. The basic thrust of that statement was that a nation's self-defense rests primarily with its own military forces; the principal role of the United States was to be the availability of its naval and air forces, in addition to its nuclear umbrella.

The question of America's willingness to fulfill its commitments to the Republic of China on Taiwan actually raises doubts about U.S. credibility in many regions. Past public-opinion polls have indicated that a substantial majority of the American people would be prepared to fight only in defense of Canada, primarily because it is a border nation; a slimmer majority would be prepared to defend one or two other nations. These polls are totally misleading, however, since on such issues public opinion is extremely mercurial. In the absence of any incident or crisis, who wants to commit himself to the awesome responsibility of war? (One recalls all of the Oxford students in Great Britain who were not going to fight in 1936.) This is not to assert that some regions of the world will not and should not weigh more heavily in American strategic thinking than others; it simply means that taking monthly polls to determine the credibility of our commitments is both foolish and dangerous. Assertions that we will not uphold our treaty commitments reduce American credibility everywhere, and raise the risk that those commitments may be tested. Moreover, such assertions are probably false, depending, of course, upon the nature of American leadership and the precise turn of events. In the event of an overt military challenge, the United States *is* likely to

respond, although not in the manner of the recent past. In the meantime, do we really want to provoke another Korea (1950) by suggesting that our current commitments are not to be trusted?

Finally, there is the thesis that by accepting China's terms for rapid normalization of relations, the United States can play a significant if not critical role in abetting moderate, rather than radical, trends within the PRC itself. This view overplays the capacities of the United States and underplays the role that indigenous Chinese forces will have in shaping future politics, domestic and foreign. If we assume that the PRC of the future will, in general, be less ideological and more "pragmatic," wedded to Chou En-lai's goal of making China a strong and prosperous nation by the end of the twentieth century, these goals will involve some support from the United States, among other foreign nations, with or without a "settlement" of the Taiwan issue. Indeed, Peking is already turning to American scientists, notably those of Chinese background, in its effort to upgrade rapidly its scientific and technological training. It has not stood back because the Taiwan issue remains unresolved—and it is not likely to do so in the future.

The question whether a strong, developing, pragmatic, nationalistic China will be a lesser or a greater threat to the rest of Asia—and to the world—than a China governed by ideology, one that truly puts politics in command, is an intriguing and complex question. In any case, Chinese goals will be determined by Chinese leaders, and with reference to China. The support of the advanced industrial societies for China's development will be forthcoming if the leadership of the PRC chooses to take advantage of it, a move that now seems likely. That, in turn, will bind the PRC more closely to these nations in certain respects; this process has characterized the USSR in recent years. Whether this situation will lead to moderation on the part of the two communist giants, as all Americans would like to believe, or to adventurism (and in the case of China, the translation of its enhanced capacities into a drive to establish a sphere of influence in southeast Asia) remains to be tested. In any case, a prudent American foreign policy will combine incentives to China, in company with other Pacific-Asian societies, to be moderate with disincentives to adventurism.

I cannot say here which of these four theses is correct, and my analysis does not claim to be a definitive one. It merely seeks to raise questions about these hypotheses that warrant consideration. Similarly, the essays that follow present various perspectives and issues in an effort to widen the discussion concerning China policy; they encompass strategic, economic, political, and ethical issues. There would be little merit in trying to summarize these essays here. They

should be read and pondered, especially by those who take other positions. Without exception, they are nonpolemical and thoughtful in character, based upon data derived from statistics and personal experience, as well as other sources; moreover, although they speak to the Taiwan issue, they also touch on some of the great dilemmas confronting those who make American foreign policy as a whole in this complex, transitional era.

1 william w. whitson

political and military dimensions

Advocates of various policies toward the Republic of China (ROC) and the People's Republic of China (PRC) do not disagree about the *ultimate* desirability of improving relations between the PRC and the United States. Policy makers disagree, however, on *how* and *when* to establish full-scale relations between the two states. These *how* and *when* issues are integral to two distinct views of political-strategic conditions throughout the world between 1945 and 1975. One view may be called "bipolar," the second "multipolar."

Those who favor the bipolar theory argue that American power was frittered away after World War II. By the late 1970s, American policy makers were being compelled to negotiate from a position of extreme weakness on issues of critical importance to the survival of American sovereignty. It is an imperative need to reverse the trend toward further diffusion of power, since it permits the United States to play only the role of "balancer" between various states. Such a role is inappropriate when the political game of the superpowers is still "zero-sum"—a life-and-death struggle requiring the mobilization of American and allied resources, not their diffusion. This school of thought would have the United States return to a posture of global leadership rather than one of uncertain partnerships.

The multipolar school, on the other hand, argues that American power was used during the Cold War to create more stable regional systems of proliferat-

ing nation-states. If American involvement in regional political issues was diminishing during the 1970s, partly by choice and partly by exclusion, the Soviet Union was similarly constrained by the working of the new international system. The major regional actors in the new system have the responsibility for resolving regional conflict, and they need time to grow accustomed to that responsibility. This school would have the United States move from world leadership toward greater regional partnership.

Recent history tends to provide support for the latter view. The thirty years between 1945 and 1975 witnessed a steady movement toward management of Asian affairs by Asians. By the late 1970s, the accumulation of power and newly won confidence by leaders *within* the subregions of Northeast, Southeast, and South Asia had provided the foundation for a uniquely Asian system of interests, values, and techniques of crisis management that was decreasingly dependent upon the involvement of the superpowers. In brief, from what had been a pale reflection of the political interests of the Atlantic community during the post–World War II period, an increasingly self-conscious and self-confident cluster of Asian political systems emerged. The promise of these regional systems is an internal process of power balancing among the large and small states of each region. In 1978, therefore, the differences of opinion about China's potential role in such a process intensified the American debate over normalization of relations with the PRC.

CHINA'S ROLE IN THE INTERNATIONAL SYSTEM

Recognizing China's evolving military and economic strength, American leaders in the Nixon administration perceived an opportunity to begin to reduce some of the dangers of bipolar confrontation between the superpowers, the United States and the Soviet Union. The effective operation of any new balance-of-power arrangement depended upon the PRC's independence of either superpower in setting its policies. Thus, the problem for American, Russian, and Chinese leaders after 1972 was to define the "appropriate political distance" among the three powers. While Secretary of State Kissinger hoped to discourage a revival of Sino-Soviet ties, he was no more enthusiastic about a close Sino-American alliance. Instead, he and Presidents Nixon and Ford urged early normalization of relations, so that the PRC might quickly play a political, if not a military-economic role, equal to those of the other two powers.

Can the PRC play such a role in the near future? Can it become a responsible actor in the Asian regional systems? Do answers to these questions depend

upon American initiatives? Or will the Chinese behave in ways dictated by their interests, and therefore ignore American policy?

The bipolarists believe that the PRC will be too weak in the short run to play a significant independent role on the world stage, especially on issues on which the superpowers might clash. Therefore, the PRC must become more closely affiliated with one of the superpowers. By working in harmony with the United States, the PRC might act as a buffer against Soviet power thrusts into the Western Pacific; it might supply natural resources, especially oil, to the United States and Japan; and it might support American initiatives in crises so that American military strength and Chinese influence might combine to block Soviet imperialism.

This school believes that Soviet power is growing rapidly in the Far East. It argues that a sense of manifest destiny among the Soviets prevents them from viewing Asia as a complex, multipolar system. Assuming that the Soviets adhere to a bipolar view of the world, they must soon either co-opt the PRC or weaken her in the global and regional political struggle. The USSR cannot tolerate the continued interference of the PRC in communist and Third-World councils as an alternative to Soviet leadership, or as an example of an alternative system and life-style for the Russian people.

Fearful of a revived Sino-Soviet entente that would pit the nations of the Eurasian land mass against a weak alliance of Western states, the bipolar school believes that there is an urgent need for a PRC-Japanese-American axis that could combine technical and human resources to contain the Soviet Union in the East just as NATO has done in the West. Such an axis could dominate the Pacific and make its political, military, and economic activities more secure. An alliance of this kind cannot be informal, however; it must be cemented with agreements, beginning with normalization of Sino-American relations.

In contrast, the multipolar school would expand on the Nixon-Kissinger initiatives without permitting the PRC to ally itself with either the USSR or the United States. Nor does this school want hostilities to break out between the PRC and Russia. Either course would destroy the balance in the triangular relationship. Between those extremes lie moderate policy options toward which the multipolar school would urge gradual and cautious movement by the United States.

Some PRC leaders are allegedly inclined to accept this position. They too prefer gradualism and experimentation in making the transition from the bipolarity of the First Cold War to the multipolarity of some new global system. From this perspective, even their concern to recover Taiwan is not as urgent a

goal as some believe. Other issues are far more important (these will be discussed below under Related Issues).

The multipolar school also contends that if the power balance among the three powers is maintained, the interests of the United States and of the PRC will converge. The Chinese will view American interests favorably without any need for a formal relationship between the two countries. Indeed the multipolar school objects to any *abrupt* change in relations between the United States and the PRC lest the Soviet response be hysterical. Its members believe that creating and maintaining a delicate balance among all three powers is more important than any short-run tactical gains by the United States over the Soviets.

THE TIMING OF NORMALIZATION OF RELATIONS

In arguments for or against the normalization of relations between the United States and the People's Republic of China, the perspectives I have just outlined on the deployment of U.S. power and the role of the PRC in international affairs are rarely made explicit. Many advocates of *early* normalization argue their case on other grounds. Similarly, advocates of delayed normalization may not necessarily be aware of the logical relationship between their arguments and the larger issues of international affairs.

Nevertheless, the timing of normalization of relations is an essential element in these perspectives. The multipolar school can be divided into two groups: those who believe that normalization should proceed gradually, and those who see no need for normalization at all. The bipolar school remains unified by a sense of urgency and by the belief that a comprehensive resolution of all outstanding issues related to PRC-U.S. relations must be hammered out very soon.

The great debate over normalization appears to be a struggle for the hearts and minds of the "gradualists" between the two extreme groups—the urgent, comprehensive school (bipolarists) and the not-now-or-necessarily-ever school (extreme multipolarists). Indeed, most discussions of normalization find the "gradualists" using reasoning similar to that of the two extreme groups. Those who would delay indefinitely see no difficulty in capturing the support of those who would delay "only a little longer," for "a little longer" obviously may be extended indefinitely. It is precisely that danger that arouses the strongest emotions in those of the urgent, comprehensive school, who argue that it is later than we think, that trends are moving faster than we think, or that the long-term consequences of our short-term procrastination will be more devastating than we think.

RELATED ISSUES

Arguments over the correct timing and technique of normalization generally center on either related issues or the Asian structure of power. Among the critical issues that are usually debated are the importance of internal stability in the PRC, the status of Taiwan, Korea, and arms control.

The internal stability of the PRC frequently figures in any debate on normalization. Does that state have the ability to mobilize its resources so that it can act responsibly and independently on the international stage?

Extremists of the multipolar school argue that the PRC would be an unreliable partner in any event. They refer to the current (1978) instability of the regime, illustrated by the ongoing struggle between the current regime and the "Gang of Four." Multipolarists therefore caution policy makers against tying American policy to a particular Peking regime, no matter how responsible or friendly it may appear to be. Any regime may change its political complexion overnight. This group also cautions against any American attempt to influence the makeup of the post-Mao leadership. Efforts to alter American policy to modulate the succession process and ensure that the PRC will maintain its strength in the superpower triangle could easily backfire and exacerbate internal rivalries in the PRC. During the transition from a Maoist era to the new one, the best policy for the United States is to ensure regional and international stability, thus buying time for the PRC to resolve its own problems.

Gradualists of the multipolar school sympathize with the latter argument. They are especially concerned about the impact of an *abrupt* American policy change in Northeast Asia that might upset the balance of power. Because they value a strong PRC as a factor in that region, they are especially sensitive to adverse consequences that might arise from the regime's domestic troubles.

On the other hand the bipolar school argues that the current "moderate" regime in the PRC desperately needs American support to demonstrate to its radical domestic opponents that ties with the West will lead to a satisfactory rate of economic development and eventual political reunification with Taiwan. The United States must act now to display goodwill toward the PRC —before the political situation there becomes even more unstable. If the United States fails to move aggressively to satisfy the PRC's demands for fulfillment of the Shanghai Communiqué, China may again be plunged into widespread violence.

This theme of China's internal *weakness* has another variation: the United States should seize the opportunity to normalize relations before the PRC becomes much stronger and more self-confident. Later the United States will

have to pay higher political, and possibly economic, costs to regain China's friendship, which the bipolarists fear is now being lost through procrastination.

The status of the ROC as a society and state usually arouses strong emotions among adversaries on the normalization issue. What of the future of Taiwan and its seventeen million people who do not wish to join the PRC? On grounds of human rights, early normalization is considered threatening to Taiwan's economy. An urgent move to normalize relations would also be a signal to investors in the ROC to withdraw, thereby weakening the confidence of business in Taiwan's future, and the ensuing flight of capital from Taiwan would further undermine confidence within the ROC. At some point bleak economic and political prospects might set off a rebellion against Mainlanders and produce a state of insurgency. Indeed, argue the multipolarists, it would be in the interest of the PRC to foment such conditions *after* normalization, for American policy would thereby be obstructed and military action by the PRC would be justified to "stabilize" the deteriorating situation on Taiwan.

This sequence of events might then encourage a strong move toward independence by the ROC, possibly encouraged by the USSR. In the view of the multipolarists, the outcome would probably be the same: American paralysis and aggressive action by the PRC to prevent an intolerable situation. An abrupt move to normalize relations, therefore, might endanger Taiwan and regional security in East Asia.

The bipolarists reject these arguments on the grounds that any adverse consequences for the ROC can be predicted and averted by American guarantees to that regime of security and investments. Indeed, arms sales by the United States to the ROC and government guarantees of current investments are already part of American policy. Agreement to such an American policy by the PRC would underline that nation's tacit, although not formal, support for peaceful resolution of the Taiwan issue.

A variation of this argument is that the United States long ago fulfilled all its obligations to Taiwan. The slate should now be cleaned; the ROC must defend itself. In any case, the PRC would be very reluctant to attack the ROC because of the high military and political costs it would incur.

The two-Koreas issue has often figured in the debate over normalization of relations with the PRC. Defenders of the status quo—the relations the United States now maintains with the PRC and the ROC—fear that sudden normalization of relations might persuade the North Koreans that the United States was no longer committed to regional security. The North Koreans might be encouraged to attack South Korea, just as the PRC might be encouraged to attack the ROC.

Advocates of normalization agree that the problem of the two Korean regimes is a related issue, but they believe that a peaceful resolution of the Korean problem is more likely if the PRC can devote its full energies to deterring North Korea. An attack by North Korea on the southern regime would not be in the interest of the PRC, but only if the problem of the ROC is removed from Peking's agenda of urgent concerns can the PRC exercise its influence to stabilize the Korean peninsula.

The issue of arms control has also been connected to the timing of normalization and the methods for achieving it. "Gradualists" believe that an urgent American move in favor of the PRC would threaten the USSR, which would harden its line on arms control and possibly rekindle the strategic-arms race. Nor would American recognition of the PRC deter the Chinese from developing their own strategic arms, because they are clearly committed to military modernization and to becoming a global power.

Advocates of normalization reject the latter argument. They believe that even if the interests of the PRC and of the United States did not converge to produce a formal alliance, the PRC would be more inclined to join strategic-arms-control agreements after friendship between the two nations had been formalized on Peking's terms. Indeed, the more moderate advocates of early recognition of the PRC by the United States argue that such a formal bilateral relationship, short of an alliance, would help reduce Soviet fears of Chinese strategic weapons and thereby facilitate progress in the U.S.-USSR SALT agreements. Failure to move soon, however, will find the Chinese becoming increasingly well-armed, possibly with SLBMs as well as ICBMs.

REGIONAL POWER STRUCTURE OF ASIA

Even if the debate ignores the outcomes of specific political issues, discussions of normalization of U.S.-PRC relations never evade the question of how power in East Asia should be distributed. The static structure of political and military power attracts more attention from analysts than the dynamics of regional political influence precisely because the structure of power seems more quantifiable and predictable than its influence.

The multipolarists plead for no *abrupt* changes in the power structure of East Asia. Even a gradual withdrawal of American political and military support for Taiwan may foster new uncertainties, revive old and new tensions, and create false expectations in Asian leaders. Any sudden rearranging of the power balance as a result of changes in American policy would certainly encourage countervailing moves that could undermine the progress achieved

through thirty years of effort in the East Asian political system. The destabiliz-
ing effect of an abrupt American move could not be corrected by the participation of the PRC as a responsible member in the East Asian community of states
because the new Sino-American alignment would demand a serious reassess-
ment of the East Asian power balance by all East Asian leaders.

The response of the bipolarists to the threat of a crumbling, unstable East
Asian power structure that might result from abrupt normalization is "why
not?" Whether by negotiation of a tight Sino-American alliance (the policy
favored by the extremists) or through recognition only (the choice of the
moderates), we must encourage the PRC to become a buffer against the
expanding might of the Soviets in Asia. We must seize every opportunity to
combine the anti-Soviet zeal of the Chinese with American material wealth
to counter the expansionist tendency of the Soviet Union. Americans would
thereby earn the PRC's gratitude and trust and, later, win the support of its
resources and manpower. The stakes are especially high (zero-sum) in the
struggle for power because the alternative to a Sino-American agreement
might be the revival of the Sino-Soviet entente.

Indeed, without quick action by the United States, Chinese leaders eventually *must* align their power with that of the USSR, thereby releasing Soviet
military power commitments in Asia and increasing its commitments to oppose
NATO and to aid friendly states in the Middle East and in Africa. Only by
moving soon can American policy makers ensure that Soviet power will remain
split between two fronts.

But as I stated above, the moderates of the multipolar school have more
respect for the PRC as an independent power than do the bipolarists. For
various ideological and political reasons, they believe that the PRC cannot
and will not lean far enough toward the USSR to recreate a Sino-Soviet
entente. The American naval and air forces currently deployed in Northeast
Asia still provide a balanced distribution of power without inciting Soviet
fears, but sudden normalization of Sino-American relations could alter this
balance in the eyes of the USSR enough to generate such fears.

Because deployed American military power is so important to the current
distribution of power in East Asia, the formation of an alliance between the
ROC and the USSR or the independent development of nuclear weapons by
the ROC would radically alter the balance of power. Such moves might
become especially important if foreign (mainly U.S. and Japanese) investments began to decline soon after normalization was achieved.

If normalization occurs without any prior consultation with other Asian
nations, Japan might become alienated from the United States and the ROC,

and might even be forced to reassess her own defenses. Normalization could warn Japan that U.S. support was no longer adequate, especially if the American military withdrawal from Korea continues on schedule. Japan might emerge as a nuclear power, or it might cave in to Soviet demands for strict neutrality regarding Sino-Soviet relations.

The bipolarists point out that Japan is already dubious about American political and military backing. The Japanese are confused; they need substantial reassurances. Only an act of strong American leadership—namely, normalization of its relations with the PRC—will remove the uncertainties in U.S.-Japanese relations and usher in a new era of even closer Sino-Japanese friendship. Foot-dragging on normalization merely weakens confidence in Japanese-American relations; thus it must be terminated. Japanese and American investments in the ROC can be protected by various political formulas. The ROC alliance is not as valuable an asset as those that can be won through closer American ties with the PRC.

THE AMERICAN MOOD IN 1978

In 1952 Frank Klingberg wrote "The Historical Alternation of Moods in American Foreign Policy."[1] He noted that the United States had experienced four periods of introversion, each averaging twenty-one years, and three periods of extroversion, each averaging twenty-eight years. He stated that the fourth period of extroversion had begun in 1940 and predicted that it would end in 1968!

There seems little doubt that American foreign policy in 1977–78 was influenced by domestic concerns with energy, employment, inflation, the environment, the credibility of government, and the general direction in which America was moving. American policy makers consciously link any China policy with the prevailing American mood. They also sense that the American people do not want any direct involvement in East Asian affairs. After all, American youth and treasure have been sacrificed in two wars fought in Asia since World War II. "Not again" is the judgment shared by the man in the street with many of his leaders.

The advocates of a cautious U.S. policy toward China point out that there is no single American political constituency demanding urgent action on normalization. After five years of foreign trade experience with the PRC, the

---

[1] Frank L. Klingberg, "The Historical Alternation of Moods in American Foreign Policy," *World Politics* 4, no. 2 (January 1952), 239–73.

business community is not enthusiastic about normalization of relations with the PRC, and those concerned about human rights hold mixed reactions about sudden normalization. Military strategists recognize China's future military capabilities, but they have not urged normalization on military-strategic grounds.

The essays that follow focus on issues the new American public opinion will very likely take into account in endorsing any new China policy: the significance of the Mutual Defense Treaty between the United States and the Republic of China; the very real human achievements on Taiwan that might be lost or dangerously eroded in the wake of premature normalization; and the potential economic costs of normalization at any price.

Each of those themes is of special importance because both separately and in combination, they remain significant components of American foreign policy in the late 1970s. The American achievement in assisting Japan, South Korea, and Taiwan to modernize and slowly evolve to more democratic policies, the American concern about human rights in East Asia, and the increasing importance of East Asian economic prosperity for the United States and the entire world deserve our attention as the United States considers the appropriate time and way to achieve more cordial relations with the People's Republic of China.

Political choices are dictated by a sense of timing in every case, and by a sense of the inevitable in many. The world changes, and with it change the symbols and uses of power. Looking at the range of foreign-policy opportunities currently confronting policy makers, future historians will probably note that the American people opposed any new American policy in East Asia that would entail abandoning Taiwan or negating its significance as a measure of American achievement in the Cold-War era—as an island bastion that stood firm against communism and forged one of the most exciting economic success stories of the Cold War. Regardless of whether the American type of democracy truly prevails in Taiwan, the opinion of the American people, confirmed by surveys in 1976 and 1977, was that America should not abandon that tiny republic.

Less systematic and precise surveys of Asian leaders (including the Peking leadership) have suggested that no East Asian leaders felt any urgency or anxiety about the normalization issue in 1978. Indeed, recent events that have taken place elsewhere in Asia, the Middle East, and Africa suggest that a decision should be delayed until the full implications of the SALT-II negotiations and the East-West trade negotiations can be assessed. Therefore, the Carter administration, which favored ultimate normalization but appreciated

those sentiments among national leaders at home and abroad, chose to postpone any action on the China question in 1977 and 1978.

The strategy now emerging seems to be one of obtaining for the United States and the PRC as many of the benefits of normalization as possible without paying the very real costs that would accompany recognition on Peking's current terms. The United States can gain substantial benefits by gradual normalization, whereas hasty moves by the president or the Congress would ensure no clear, short-term political advantage and might even create turmoil at home (certainly they would do so for investors in Taiwan) and very likely produce high risk and uncertainty for businessmen and governments in East Asia.

2 norma schroder

economic costs and benefits

Since early 1972 the United States has enjoyed economic relations with both Chinese regimes. American trade and investment in the ROC has flourished since World War II, particularly because of the free-market conditions in both countries and the laws that protect and favor trader and investor alike. Trade between the United States and the PRC has just commenced, but it always will be strongly influenced by the inherent characteristics of the PRC's economy: pervasive state controls and planning policies that affect the economic system's potential to export and import.

Trade between the United States and the PRC in the near future can be further expanded by concluding various political-economic agreements that fall short of establishing full diplomatic relations between the two: settlement of the "frozen-assets" issue to allow conventional banking and shipping relations to expand; negotiation of a trade agreement granting most-favored-nation status to Chinese goods entering the United States; and a bilateral agreement concerning the protection of proprietary rights such as patents, copyrights, and trademarks.

Unlike diplomatic recognition of the PRC on that country's present terms, these recommended legal changes would not impose economic costs on third parties such as Taiwan and its Asian and American trading partners.[1] What

---

[1] Although treatment of the PRC as a most-favored nation would impose some costs on the Southest Asian nations who already have this status by diminishing their differential tariff advantage, these nations applaud commercial fairness and presumably would welcome this move, which would reconfirm U.S. endorsement of the principles of competitive fairness in world trade.

are some of the economic benefits the United States currently enjoys in its relations with both the ROC and the PRC? What are some of the difficulties that will always hinder trade between the United States and the PRC even after normalization of relations between the two countries has been achieved? What will be some of the economic costs for the United States if it severs its relationships with the ROC? This essay provides some answers to these questions and further argues that current U.S. economic ties with both China regimes can be expanded—even short of U.S.-PRC normalization—to the benefit of all parties.

ECONOMIC RELATIONS BETWEEN THE UNITED STATES AND THE REPUBLIC OF CHINA

Since 1952 the economy of the ROC has been characterized by rapid, sustained economic growth. Its per-capita rate of real gross national product (GNP) growth until 1972 (the year of the oil crisis) was 5.6 percent, exceeding that of virtually every other developing nation, including the PRC (in 1977 the CIA estimated that since 1957 the annual rate of real GNP growth in the PRC had been slightly more than 3 percent). In 1977 the ROC's per-capita income reached nine hundred U.S. dollars, placing it among Asia's top five nations; income distribution in that country has also become more equal. In 1953 the top 20 percent of all households, ranked by income, received 61 percent of total income; by 1972 this top group's share had shrunk to 39 percent.[2] A variety of reforms and government policies to modulate the private sector's economic performance has contributed to this dynamic record of economic growth.

Before the 1972–74 world recession, U.S. imports from East and Southeast Asia (excluding Japan) were growing at an annual rate of 16 percent, a much higher rate than that of U.S. imports from the developing nations as a whole (14.4 percent), and a higher rate than that of U.S. imports from all nations (14.6 percent). Over that period our imports from the ROC grew at the impressive rate of 39 percent. Table 1 presents the annual growth rates of U.S. imports from, exports to, and direct investments in the ROC and major world regions between 1960 and 1974.

---

[2] Scholars disagree on when income distribution became more equal and the extent to which equality was achieved. For the best analysis, see Han-yu Chang, "Income Disparity under Economic Growth in Taiwan over Time Changes and Degree as Compared with Other Countries," *Industry of Free China*, June 1977, pp. 2–17.

TABLE 1

CONSTANT ANNUAL GROWTH RATES OF U.S. IMPORTS FROM, EXPORTS TO, AND DIRECT
INVESTMENT IN THE ROC AND MAJOR WORLD REGIONS, 1960–1974

	(1) U.S. Imports from (percent)	(2) U.S. Exports to (percent)	(3) U.S. Net Capital Flow (percent)
Republic of China	38.99	12.39	28.31
East and Southeast Asia	16.16	10.73	32.22
Japan	18.56	14.43	10.82
Developing Nations	14.42	11.49	13.69
Developed Nations	14.62	11.73	6.78
All Nations	14.58	11.83	9.02

SOURCE: Author's computation based on Commerce Department data in *Survey of Current Business,*
August issues from 1960 through 1974. Country groupings were changed after 1974, making it impossible
to extend the series to the present.

In the early 1950s, when Taiwan exported mainly sugar, the country was of little trade significance to the United States, but by the mid-1970s Taiwan had become the seventh largest source of U.S. imports, outranking France as a supplier. Taiwan's exports to Japan, Asia, and the European Economic Community (Common Market) have also expanded rapidly, but the United States remains its largest market. In 1977 the United States absorbed about 40 percent of Taiwan's exports, while second-ranked Japan took only 13.5 percent. The United States and other nations have increased their purchases from the ROC, such as textiles and electrical supplies, because of their high quality and low price.

The annual rate of growth of the East and Southeast Asian market for U.S. exports, 10.7 percent, has been below that of all nations combined (11.8 percent). The growth rate of the ROC market (12.4 percent) has topped that of all nations, although it trails the Japan market's growth rate of 14.4 percent. By the mid-1970s the ROC was the tenth largest purchaser of U.S. exports, outranking Switzerland and Israel. It is expected to rise to sixth place in a few years.

The striking fact about direct investments by the United States in East and Southeast Asia is that they have been growing at more than twice the annual rate of U.S. investments in developing countries (32 percent compared with 13.7 percent). The annual growth rate of American capital invested in the ROC (28.2 percent) makes that nation one of the most attractive investment recipients in Asia. U.S. capital has been deployed to Asia at high growth rates

because that is where investors have enjoyed superlative sales volume and profits. Between 1966 and 1972, U.S. multinational corporations experienced their most rapid growth in sales in Asia (including Japan, New Zealand, and Australia). Prior to the post-1972 world recession, the rate of return on U.S. direct investment in manufacturing in the Far East was nearly 23 percent, whereas the average rate of return for its investments in all nations was 16 percent, and Latin America offered a return of only 13 percent.

Meanwhile loans from U.S. banks to the ROC remain strong. The U.S. Export-Import Bank alone has extended more than $1 billion in loans to the ROC and has guaranteed another $700 million in private bank loans. This makes the ROC that bank's third largest customer, trailing only Brazil and Spain. In late March, 1977, the Export-Import Bank granted loans totalling $1.54 billion to the China Steel Corporation, the Chinese Petroleum Corporation, the Taiwan Railway Administration, and the Taiwan Power Company (which planned to use its loan funds to construct a nuclear power plant). Credit from this bank now supplies American firms in the ROC with $2.5 billion worth of business.

America's economic stakes in the ROC are high: it has made direct investments there totalling nearly $500 million; its manufacturing subsidiaries enjoy among the highest rates of profitability and sales growth in the world; and the ROC is its thirteenth-ranked trading partner.

TRADE RELATIONS AND PROSPECTS OF TRADE BETWEEN THE UNITED STATES AND THE PRC

Unlike the rapidly expanding trade relations between the United States and the ROC, economic relations between the United States and the PRC have proven to be unstable. This instability does not originate from the current political relations between the two countries, but from the stop-gap role exports play in correcting "mistakes" in a planned economy and the recent poor performance of the PRC's economy. Table 2 shows trade between the United States and the PRC from 1971 to early 1977.

In the Chinese planned economy, imports are a policy instrument used: (1) to ease pressure on the domestic transport and distribution system, especially by supplying grain to coastal cities; (2) to correct planning errors leading to poor harvests and underinvestment in lagging sectors; and (3) to accelerate economic growth by importing capital goods the PRC cannot produce itself.

In 1972 the Chinese purchased ten Boeing 707s, and in 1973 and 1974 they

TABLE 2

TRADE BETWEEN THE UNITED STATES AND THE PEOPLE'S REPUBLIC OF CHINA
(millions of U.S. $)

Year	U.S. Exports	U.S. Imports	Total	U.S. Balance
1971	0	4	4	—4
1972	63	32	95	+31
1973	690	64	754	+626
1974	819	115	934	+704
1975	304	158	462	+146
1976	135	201	336	—66
1977 (Jan.–July)	68	116	184	—48

SOURCE: "China's Economy," National Foreign Assessment Center of the CIA, November 1977, p. 10.

relied upon large capital imports from various nations to expand domestic steel and chemical-fertilizer production. They spent U.S. $1.3 billion in 1973 and another $0.8 billion in 1974 for the Wuhan steel complex, which was built by Italy and West Germany, and for eight fertilizer plants constructed by the M. W. Kellogg corporation of Houston, Texas. Table 2 clearly shows that these were the golden years for trade between the United States and the PRC. Many thought that this interest by the Chinese in high-technology projects might lead to further major purchases from the United States and other producers, but Chinese bids for new capital from abroad declined rapidly after 1974. The PRC cut back its new purchases in 1976 partly because 23 percent of the hard currency it earned on its 1975 exports was already committed to debt repayments stemming from capital purchases made in 1972–73. Further, the debt obligations stemming from the emergency purchase of 6.5 million tons of grain for delivery in 1977 had forced the PRC to sell gold to supplement its hard-currency earnings from its 1976–77 exports. Finally, fluctuating grain harvests have compelled the Chinese to buy wheat abroad. In 1973 footstuffs comprised more than 60 percent of American exports to China and in 1974 more than 40 percent. PRC grain imports surged again in 1977 because of harvest difficulties and disruptions of railway services.

In other words, the sudden decline in trade between the United States and the PRC after 1974 seems to have originated not in obstacles to normalization of relations but in the inability of the PRC to increase its exports because of domestic scarcities and bottlenecks, the difficulties of financing capital imports

on a sustained basis because of the rise in the loan repayment/export ratio, and the failure to achieve self-sufficiency in grain, which led to the spending of foreign exchange for foreign grain purchases. (China probably will not hesitate to use the United States as a residual supplier of foodstuffs during any bad harvest years, regardless of whether normalization occurs soon or in the distant future. In April 1978 there were reports of large grain purchases from the United States by the PRC.)

A more serious problem for China's foreign trade, particularly that country's capacity to deal with the United States, is whether its economy can produce enough export growth to bring in substantial capital from abroad. Consider the following hypothetical example recently advanced by a U.S. government economist, David L. Denny. Denny assumed that after actually spending $1.3 billion on plant purchases in 1973, the PRC would continue to spend $1 billion on plants annually through 1982, and that these purchases would be financed by medium-term credit beginning after the construction was completed—within two to three years after the signing of the contract. Denny then predicted the following repayment difficulties for the PRC:

> The result is a steady rise in the PRC repayment schedule [excluding agricultural repayments] to about $1.2 billion in 1980. To maintain a relatively conservative debt repayment ratio of 15 percent, PRC exports to the non-communist countries would have to rise to $8 billion by 1980. Since such exports are already $3.9 in 1973, this would require them to grow 10 percent annually. . . . Even if payment for contracted agricultural products [up to and including 1973's purchases but excluding the unexpected bulge in 1977 deliveries, which Denny did not know about in 1973] were included, the repayment schedule would amount to only $2 billion in most years. A 20 percent debt service ratio might be maintained by a quite reasonable export growth of about 12 percent per year. Their inclusion does point up what may be a difficult short-term liquidity problem for the PRC. Depending on the exact size and timing of agricultural repayments, it may be difficult to keep the debt service ratio from rising beyond 20 percent.[3]

This is not to say that China cannot exceed the 20 percent "ceiling," should it choose, if exports fail to expand at or above the annual rate of 10 percent, but it would have to abandon its "pay-as-you-go" approach to buying abroad.

Chinese acceptance of longer-term credit on any particular group of projects is a distinct future possibility, especially as the new leadership in 1978 has

---

[3] David L. Denny, "Recent Development in the International Financial Policies of the People's Republic of China," *China's Changing Role in the World Economy*, edited by Bryant G. Garth and the editors of the *Stanford Journal of International Studies* (New York: Praeger, 1975), p. 180.

expressed its commitment to making China a modern economic power by the end of this century. The PRC's new economic projections call for industrial growth accelerating to 10 percent per annum and agricultural growth increasing to 4 percent per annum, targets that are well within the realm of possibility provided key scarcities can be eliminated and political stability and unity can be guaranteed. The question remains, of course, to what extent China's limited technological infrastructure can absorb sudden new infusions of capital. Hopes were recently expressed in the West that banks could expand direct loans to the Chinese to finance their purchases, but these were quashed in October 1977 when Vice–Foreign Minister Yu Chan flatly stated that China would not resort to foreign loans.

There have been other difficulties too, including certain commercial practices connected with U.S.-PRC trade that have prevented that trade from expanding more rapidly than it has. Again, it must be noted that these practices have nothing to do with the thorny issue of normalization, but are rooted in the cultural and business practices of both nations.

Contract negotiations for sales to or purchases from China have been an arduous, frustrating experience for most Western businessmen.[4] Many complain that a long stay at the Canton Trade Fair increases the cost of their purchases from China and frequently forces them to lose opportunities for profit elsewhere. Furthermore, unless they place large orders, they are not assured of being reinvited to the fair.

Western sales representatives sometimes lament that they must deal with intermediaries—agents of the State Trading Agency—rather than with the "end users" and that they are thus at a disadvantage in successfully consummating sales. Similarly, Western buyers can blame China's unwillingness to restyle, package, and label Chinese exports for their particular market segment partly on the State Trading Agency, which bars access to discussions with "end suppliers." The inflexibility in product design may be attributed to the lack of exposure of the Chinese to ordinary marketing tactics in a modern mixed economy and their failure to grasp the faddishness of Western, especially American, consumer tastes. This situation may be changing for the better, though. The experience of the 1976 fall and 1977 spring fairs suggests that the exhortations of the new Peking leaders to the Chinese to export more are having an ameliorative effect at the level of actual trading operations. "Chinese

---

[4] These observations are based on Stanley Lubman, "Trade with the United States," in *Law and Politics in China's Foreign Trade*, edited by V. H. Li (Seattle: University of Washington Press, 1977) pp 220–46.

suppliers were eager to do business and were quite amenable to buyers' requests on labeling styles and packaging." [5]

Just as the Chinese are slow to respond to the dictates of a changing market, so they are either oblivious or insensitive to Western market pricing conventions. Chinese pricing policy does not conform to the Western practice of setting a wholesale-retail price differential, which is intrinsic to our distribution system. Instead, both wholesalers and retailers (who are not permitted to bring the large numbers of specialized buyers they rely on to the fair) must buy at identical prices. "Yet the prices are so high that wholesalers have difficulty in making their customary mark-up when selling to retailers." [6]

Chinese practices are rigid with respect to quantities as well as prices. Minimum-order requirements as well as rules stipulating the filling up of standard Chinese sizes of packing cases eliminate small-quantity buyers and sample orders. Ironically, very large orders are not possible either. "Several representatives of potentially large American buyers have left Canton having bought little or nothing after discovering that the Chinese output of the products they wanted was too small for the Chinese to be able to sell the quantities they desired." [7] Stanley Lubman has called the Canton Trade Fair "a gigantic exercise in the allocation of Chinese exports," where Americans are told that "old friends" must be accommodated first, and where regular European customers are told not to expect the accustomed allotments because China has "new friends."

Once the businessman has survived the onerous negotiation of a sales contract with the Chinese, he must run the gauntlet of the Chinese international-payments mechanism. The Chinese almost always prefer to use the payments instrument known as the letter of credit, even though it is both inconvenient and expensive to amend the letter because of changes in shipping dates. When the Chinese buy goods from abroad, they typically open their letters of credit fifteen to thirty days in advance of the shipping date; when Westerners buy from China, however, the Chinese require the foreign purchaser to open their letters of credit as much as sixty to ninety days in advance of the shipping date. This means that Western working capital is tied up substantially longer than Chinese.

Another difficulty is that of which party will bear the foreign-exchange risk of a transaction. Unlike other developing countries with inconvertible

---

[5] "China: International Trade 1976–77," *National Foreign Assessment Center of the CIA*, November 1977, p. 6.

[6] Lubman, "Trade," p. 231.

[7] Ibid., p. 229.

currencies that denominate their sales in an international currency, since 1968 China has almost always denominated its sales in *Renminbi* (RMB) ; thus, the buyer does not know the dollar cost of his purchases until the products he has contracted for are ready for shipment. The Bank of China does enable some European buyers to hedge their goods purchases against a revaluation of RMB by offering advance contracts for sales of RMB (at rather expensive interest rates—3–6 percent), but these contracts are available to Americans only in commercially insignificant amounts.[8] "Even then the purchase cannot be made . . . by the third country bank in the United States which has been handling the financial arrangements [of the businessman seeking advance contracts for RMB] . . . unless the American purchaser prepays the credit, thereby tying up his working capital for months."[9] Ironically, when the PRC has denominated its purchases in dollars, the fluctuations of the foreign-exchange market have worked to its gain. For example, in 1972, early in the U.S.-PRC trade boomlet, the Chinese made several major purchases that were denominated in dollars instead of RMB, and because the value of the dollar declined after the contracts were drawn up, they acquired these goods more cheaply than they would have if they had been denominated in RMB.

Thus far we have followed the Western (American) businessman through the contract stage and the payments stage of his trade transaction with China. If something goes wrong at this point, several clauses that he conceded in the original sales contract come into play. Because Americans must open their letters of credit much earlier than the Chinese, shipping delays have a much worse effect on them. When Americans are buying, their working capital can be tied up for extra weeks and months; although the Chinese realize the burden a delay puts on Americans, they will not provide any recompense until the buyer reappears at the next Canton Fair, and then they offer compensation only on an ad-hoc basis—for instance, by upping the buyer's allotment of goods, shaving the price, or being more cooperative in product styling. In contrast, when delays occur in the shipment of Western goods to China, the Chinese claim formalized recompense via the penalties clause that has invariably been inserted in their standard sales contract.

Once the goods arrive, the risks and costs associated with deviations from the specified quality are also different for the Americans and the Chinese. If the Chinese Bureau of Commodity Inspection has certified that a Chinese export shipment meets specifications, the Western purchaser generally has no

---

[8] Denny, "Recent Development," p. 236.
[9] Lubman, "Trade," p. 236.

recourse if he finds defects upon receipt of the goods. Sometimes arbitration clauses are included in contracts, but most traders have been reluctant to use them because the Chinese regard such requests for arbitration as "unfriendly." Instead, at the next fair the aggrieved Westerner is asked to settle for the same kinds of ad-hoc adjustments to his order that are offered in compensation for shipping delays. The Bureau of Commodity Inspection has the last word on Chinese shipments of foodstuffs, too. The Chinese have adamantly refused to assume responsibility for the rejection of food by the Food and Drug Administration. They consider many FDA tests capricious, such as the olfactory one for shrimp. On the other hand, this same bureau can be very exacting about very minor variations from the contract specifications in Western shipments. Many defects that are usually overlooked, such as hairline cracks in rolled steel, are likely to give rise to Chinese claims. The Chinese adamantly refused several wheat shipments from the United States in 1974 because of the existence of TCK (Tilletia controversa K.), a fungus causing dwarf smut.

ECONOMIC EFFECTS OF NORMALIZATION OF U.S.-PRC RELATIONS

The volume of new direct investments in the ROC by the United States and Japan has fluctuated with the republic's political fortunes. The ROC's departure from the United Nations in 1971 and Japan's recognition of the PRC in 1972 caused substantial dips in the flow of new investments, and the effects of this drop were compounded by the ongoing worldwide recession. If the ROC were to fall into international limbo because of normalization of relations between the United States and the PRC on Peking's terms, the future status of American businesses in the ROC would become most uncertain. Some of the unknowns that might adversely affect American investment are as follows:

Will American business continue to enjoy national treatment in the hands of the ROC government? . . . Will the various insurance schemes against incontrovertibility and expropriation offered by the U.S. government and its agencies continue to be valid? What will be the proper procedure to resolve questions, or to settle disputes, that may arise in present or future contracts or in the course of doing business (e.g. in the case of oil spills by one party's tankers in the territorial waters of the other).[10]

---

[10] Y. S. Wu and K. C. Yeh, "The Economic Impact of Alternative US-ROC Relations," *International Trade Law Journal* 3, no. 1 (Fall 1977), p. 158.

Such uncertainties could induce investors either to stay away altogether or at least to avoid the long-term commitments they would have made if they had faced only ordinary business risks (these risks have always been lower in the ROC than in other developing countries because of the ROC's remarkable stability and prosperity).

The growth of exports from the ROC might be adversely affected if foreign direct investment suddenly declined. Reduced earnings from exports might compel the ROC to increase its foreign borrowings to finance the capital imports that are necessary to achieve current growth-rate targets. The increased loan burden might push the ROC to the sound-debt-service ceiling of 20 percent, thereby constraining economic growth. As of 1977 the ROC's ratio (6 percent) was among the lowest in the developing world!

If the ROC were to enter international political limbo, a myriad of issues could affect its foreign trade.

> For instance, would Taiwan continue to enjoy Most-Favored-Nation status in the United States and other markets? Would Export-Import Bank facilities continue to be available to private and public ROC firms? Would Taiwan benefit under the General Preference Scheme of tariff reductions? Would ROC flag ships and aircraft be able to function in foreign countries without interference and delay? Would ROC government and private interests be able to exploit resources in the deep sea and on the continental shelf under whatever protection international law normally provides? Would ROC fishing vessels be able to operate in ever-widening areas as they do now? ... Can visa application by ROC businessmen and other travellers be processed quickly? Would contractual obligations between ROC and other nationals be enforceable and in what court?[11]

Court tests and administrative interpretations of ambiguous regulations and statutes would spell delays that would raise the costs of conducting business with the ROC, and thereby dim the profit prospects for American traders.

Furthermore, limbo status for the ROC would enable third parties to apply unfair pressure more effectively and to curtail relations between the ROC and the rest of the world. Two examples serve to demonstrate that this fear is not unfounded:

> 1. A message ... ostensibily originat[ing] from the China council for the Promotion of International Trade in Peking ... was delivered to the president of the National Council for US-China Trade by a member of the PRC Liaison Office in Washington in May 1976 to the effect that US firms might find their

---

[11] Ibid., p. 13.

trade with the PRC adversely affected by their membership in a recently formed US-ROC Economic Council.

2. According to a *Los Angeles Times* report on September 8, 1976, several U.S. firms had been targets of PRC discrimination in their trade probes because of their attempts to do business with both Taiwan and the Mainland.[12]

Taiwanese businessmen and industrialists have been complaining about discrimination by Common Market countries and have said that they were loath to spend any more money trying to broaden their European markets.

Two conclusions can be reached based on the information given above. In spite of the shocks the ROC suffered as a result of international events in the early 1970s, its economy has so far weathered the adjustments demanded of it. Nevertheless, the economic uncertainties likely to arise if the United States suddenly severs its ties with the ROC to satisfy the demands of the PRC are real enough. The possibility always exists that much of the Taiwanese managerial and capitalist classes would abandon the ROC if widespread pandemonium should erupt—in response to an apparent abandonment of the ROC leadership by the United States. Such a hemorrhage of human and financial capital would not require an actual takeover of that regime by the PRC, but only a belief by the Taiwanese that immediate threat of takeover existed. Thus the possibility of a decline in foreign direct investments that would adversely influence exports and imports, and ultimately economic growth itself, remains and must be taken seriously.

CONCLUSION

The economic benefits of U.S. trade with and direct investments in the ROC have grown and can be expected to continue as long as stability can be maintained in the region. The United States has also received modest benefits from a brief flurry of U.S. and PRC trade; although it has since subsided, the prospects for a renewed exchange are not gloomy. Certain concrete steps might be undertaken to encourage such a revival. First, we can settle the "frozen-assets" issue, which because of the fear of attachment of property precludes direct shipping and banking relations and thereby raises the costs of trading with China. Second, we can forge a bilateral agreement to protect literary and industrial property—copyrights, patents, and trademarks. Third, we can develop a trade arbitration mechanism to settle disputes over shipping delays and quality deviations.

---

[12] Ibid., p. 15.

These measures could be realized by negotiating an overall trade agreement. There are precedents: China has concluded trade agreements with several European nations with which no formal diplomatic relations existed at the time (West Germany, Denmark, and Italy). The language of the U.S. legislation concerning such a bilateral agreement, the Trade Reform Act of 1974, suggests that the negotiation process will not be easy because it cannot be unilateral:

> In the Trade Reform Act of 1974, Congress enacted legislation which *requires* the President to receive concessions from any Communist nation in return for an agreement to extend Most-Favored-Nation treatment to the nation's products ...and a Chinese agreement to extend Most-Favored-Nation treatment to American imports is no concession at all, since China is a state-trading nation. ... [Presumably China could make non-tariff concessions though] Congress [in the Jackson-Vanek amendment] also made Chinese policies toward emigration into a trade-related issue by enacting general language applicable to all Communist countries, which restrains the President from negotiating an agreement unless he certifies that the emigration policy of the country in question meets certain standards.[13]

The requirement of emigration certification will be a sticking point with the Chinese as it was with the USSR, but it is one Congress has the option of removing unilaterally if the consensus is that expanded trade with China is more important than imposing on China our own values on the human-rights issue.

Abandonment of the emigration requirement, which would probably be necessary to forge a bilateral trade agreement with China, can do as much to expand trade between the United States and the PRC as capitulation on the Taiwan security issue—and in the author's opinion at much less cost. It seems unlikely that normalization of relations between the United States and the PRC on China's terms would produce a trade agreement very different from one that could be developed without downgrading relations between the United States and the ROC.

> If and when normalization [were to] occur, the prospects would be for a slow evolution rather than a dramatic leap forward [in commercial relations]. But the normalization would signal the commencement of a new stage in Sino-American relations which would probably be reflected in trade as well, both in volume and the articulation of an institutional framework for trade. Yet even

---

[13] Lubman, "Trade," p. 246.

then, the commercial practices which China has developed in the course of long years of trade with Western partners and Japan are unlikely to be dramatically altered.[14]

If normalization of relations with the PRC will not dramatically alter the situation, why not expand the volume of trade and establish an institutional framework with the PRC by using the less costly (to Taiwan and its American and Asian trading partners) bilateral trade agreement instead? There may be some sentiment in Peking for doing just that. For instance, in September 1977 Party Vice-Chairman and preeminent economic planner Li Hsien-nien told American journalists that the claims-and-assets problem, which prevented a full-scale U.S.-PRC trade relationship, could be solved before the thorny Taiwan issue was resolved.[15]

---

[14] Ibid., p. 246.
[15] *Far Eastern Economic Review, Asia Yearbook 1978* (Hong Kong, 1978), p. 26.

3 the human dimension

c. martin wilbur

When I first visited Taipei in 1954 it was an easygoing, rather slipshod provincial city. On the streets one saw many pedicab drivers sleeping or loitering. "Where is the energy?" I wrote in my journal. "Is there a drive toward modernization, toward economic expansion?" When I was there in 1961 the pace had quickened, but street traffic was still bumbling and confused; I saw a mixture of bicycles, pedicabs, a few trucks, cars and buses, and an occasional oxcart lumbering by.

How could I doubt the "drive" of Taipei? For today, Taipei suffers from the frenzied transportation network characteristic of any modern urban center. Motorcycles, both Taiwan-built models and the popular Japanese ones, are now the main privately owned means of transportation—more than one for every ten persons. They roar down on slow-footed pedestrians like a pack of wolves; and for many blocks in downtown Taipei they are parked so tightly side by side on the sidewalks that it is hard to squeeze through them to the curb. Most people use the efficient system of public buses, which traverse all parts of the city and connect it with other urban centers. If a visitor wishes to escape the crowd, he has only to hail one of the many small taxicabs that dart in and

This chapter was completed in October 1977, and updated somewhat in April 1978. Statistics are derived mainly from *Taiwan Statistical Data Book 1977*, published by the Economic Planning Council, Executive Yuan of the Government of the Republic of China, in June 1977.

out of traffic to take him speedily where he wants to go.

The ramshackle wood or mud-brick shops and dwellings of twenty years ago are now being replaced by eight- to ten-story office buildings and four-story, concrete apartment buildings with terraces. Today the implementation of comprehensive city plans and the enterprise of private builders are changing the face of the capital city. The city planners have slashed through the aging, poorly built neighborhoods with broad paved boulevards that radiate outward toward the suburban villages, many of which have already been gobbled up by the city sprawl. At present, this city which attracts thousands of new emigrants each year has an insatiable demand for more and better dwelling units—a demand the speculative builders are rushing to meet, despite the risks. In each section of the city, bamboo scaffolding and construction crews can be found everywhere.

Twenty years ago household goods and modern services were in very short supply in Taipei; now they are abundant. Consumerism has gripped the nation. Two out of every three families in Taiwan own television sets, and they get a regular diet of consumer-goods advertising that is as blatant as the fare in Japan or the West. The shopper can satisfy his appetite for goods at many department stores, in the crowded two-level Chung-hua Bazaar, or at the new multistoried Western-style shopping complex outfitted with escalators and "boutiques." Fashion-conscious men and women can browse among the racks of ready-to-wear clothing of various colors, fabrics, and contemporary Western styles. Blue jeans and short skirts have captured the young. Electrical appliances of good quality—fans, air conditioners, lamps, calculators—that were once unknown or scarce, are now widely displayed in downtown stores as well as in small neighborhood shops.

Businesses catering to leisure pursuits are thriving. Bookstores are filled with books, magazines, and buyers. The theaters, which typically run the popular kung-fu, war, romantic, or Hong Kong–made kung-fu movies in addition to an occasional older American flick, are ordinarily filled to capacity. Beauty parlors will pamper a lady's tresses before a special dinner date for a modest fee. Dining out has also become extremely popular: medium-grade restaurants are packed. Tea houses, once places for men of leisure to go for a few hours of social or business conversation, now have all the chairs facing one way—toward the television set; patrons gaze silently at the Chinese soap operas or traditional theatricals that flash before their eyes both afternoon and evening.

Children in Taiwan are delightful. I was repeatedly struck by the affectionate way in which Chinese parents treat their little children. It is common to see a father on a bus dandling his baby on his knee, patting and kissing him, or

families in a park with parents hugging their little children. They raise their cherished toddlers in the traditional, gentle manner, which is permissive even by Western standards. Then, as the youngsters grow to school age, the screws of discipline are tightened and parents exhort their offspring to study hard and improve their status. On any morning early you can see droves of bright-faced kids in freshly laundered uniforms strolling off to primary school. When they reach middle-school age, academic competition becomes intense, and the young folks study late into the night. With college—or emancipation from study for those who do not go on—comes another time of relaxation. It is a period of enjoyment, devoted to rapping and dating, but this time minus the uniform.

Permit one more personal impression. In 1962, after eight months in Taiwan, where most of my friends were of the academic world, I wrote in my journal that none of them could depend upon his teaching salary alone. They had to find extra jobs—teaching and magazine writing—to cover three-fifths of their living expenses. They met this situation with stoic fortitude, yet I sensed a mood of despair under the bright exterior. Now all that has changed. My friends tell me that academic salaries are fully adequate. A husband and wife who both work can save a lot. Many of my academic friends own their apartments now, with modern kitchens, well-stocked refrigerators, and up-to-date bathrooms.

ADVANCES IN SOCIAL WELFARE

"A nation's most valuable resource is its people, and the future of a nation lies with its youth." Both officials and parents in the Republic of China believe in the validity of this aphorism. Accordingly, many social programs have been implemented in Taiwan—family planning, public health, manpower planning and carefully constructed education, employment insurance and provision of pensions, to name a few.

Taiwan's growing population and the rising expectations of its people create many problems. The island is only 250 miles long and 90 to 120 miles across in the wider places. Only about one quarter of its 13,800 square miles are arable. Thus its nearly seventeen million people—about twice the combined populations of Massachusetts and Connecticut—are crowded into a smaller area. More than 60 percent of the Taiwanese live in cities: Taipei already has more than two million inhabitants.

Taiwan is now a healthful place to live. Daily per-capita calorie intake increased from 2,078 to 1952 to 2,701 in 1976. In 1970, Taiwan was ahead of Japan, the Republic of Korea, Thailand, and the Philippines among East Asian countries in this respect (I have not seen comparable figures for the People's Republic of China). Daily per-capita protein intake increased from an average of 49.0 grams per day in 1952 to 74.8 grams in 1976. Increasing amounts of milk are being consumed by young folks in cities. As a result of better diet, children have gained in average height and weight, and their life expectancy has greatly increased. I was truly impressed by the sturdy boys and girls I saw in Taipei in the summer of 1977.

Seven types of contagious disease have been eliminated from the island. Malaria has been wiped out, though in the first few years after Taiwan returned to Chinese control there were more than a million cases each year. There were no reported cases of smallpox and only two cases of scarlet fever between 1966 and 1977. A cholera epidemic in 1962 caused twenty-four deaths, but no cases have appeared since then. The incidence of typhoid and paratyphoid, diphtheria, dysentery, and epidemic cerebrospinal meningitis has been greatly reduced during the past decade.

By 1976 the total number of registered medical personnel (physicians, herbalists, dentists and dental assistants, pharmacists and their assistants, nurses, midwives, and laboratory workers) had increased nearly sixfold since 1952—a period during which the population only doubled. The greatest increases have been in the numbers of physicians, pharmacists, and nurses. There is a hospital bed for each 503 persons (the figure for Japan is 103), and a physician for each 1,437. Because of improved maternal and infant health care, infant mortality dropped from 44.7 per thousand live births in 1952 to 12.9 in 1974. In the same period, maternal deaths also declined sharply—from nearly 13 per thousand deliveries to 0.32.

Nevertheless, health care is not distributed evenly among the urban and rural populations, a disparity that is found in most countries. The province has 347 rural health stations, but they suffer from a shortage of qualified physicians. While there is no program of paramedical personnel similar to the institution of the famous "barefoot doctors" in the PRC, Taiwan's National Health Administration and its provincial government are implementing a plan to set up ten new medical-service stations and to form mobile medical teams to serve people in remote areas.

Because of the excellent network of public-health facilities, as well as a marked improvement in diet, the annual crude death rate was cut in half between 1952 and 1977. On the average, children born in Taiwan today may

expect to live twelve years longer than their parents born twenty-five years earlier—to age 68.4 for males and 73.4 for females. (Comparable figures for the United States are age 68.2 for males and 75.9 for females; for Mexico they are age 62.8 for males and 66.6 for females.)

The *rate* of population growth has declined gradually over the past twenty-five years, partly because of increasing prosperity, higher literacy rates, and urbanization, and partly because of a vigorous program by the government to encourage family planning. The program includes counseling, distribution of contraceptives, and facilities for voluntary sterilization after optimum family size is achieved, as well as an island-wide educational campaign on the dangers of overpopulation. The Taipei Family Planning Promotion Center conducts lectures, group discussions, and exhibitions; presents movies and issues leaflets and posters; and presses the message of family planning by television, radio, newspaper, and bus advertising.

The provincial Family Planning Promotion Center in Taichung has a similar program, inaugurated in 1964, though it is more difficult to spread the message to rural folk and to convince them of the desirability of small families. Public-health stations, middle schools and junior colleges, and the network of farmers' associations all assist in the effort. Since 1964, when a program of population control became national policy, the rate of population growth has declined from more than 3 percent a year to 1.8 percent and 1.9 percent in 1974 and 1975; in 1976, "the year of the dragon," however, the rate jumped to 2.2 percent, allegedly because Chinese have traditionally considered it very lucky for boys to be born in that year.

The reduction in the growth rate since 1965 has been a notable achievement, but the higher birth rates of the 1950s meant that increasing numbers of people have been entering the work force in the 1970s. Furthermore, the percentage of workers in agriculture, forestry, and fishing has been declining—from 43.4 percent in 1966 to 29.1 percent in 1976. In the industrializing economy, ever-increasing numbers are employed in manufacturing, commerce, and services. The Six-Year Plan for Economic Development of Taiwan projects a population of just under eighteen million in mid-1981.

The Republic of China provides the 27 percent of the population who are of school age with a system of free education for nine years; the first six years are compulsory. In the 1976–77 school year, 99.42 percent of the children aged six to twelve were enrolled in primary schools and 91 percent of the graduates went on to junior high school. Given the growing population, the achievement of nearly universal free education with an enrollment of 3,857,000 children

has required a huge investment in new schools and in teacher training. Enrollments at all levels of education totalled nearly 4.5 million in 1977, almost 35 percent of the population.

The secondary educational system consists of three-year senior high schools and three-year vocational schools. There were eleven times as many students at this level in 1976–77 as there were in 1952–53. The vocational school system was expanded in response to the need for more technically trained persons for industry. In 1976–77, 260,000 students were enrolled in commercial and industrial high schools.

The most dramatic educational development has been the increase in the number of colleges and students in higher education. In 1952–53 Taiwan had only 8 institutions for higher education; twenty-five years later there were 101, of which 9 were universities, 16 were colleges, and 76 were junior colleges. The number of students in them grew from a little over 10,000 to just under 300,000, a thirtyfold increase, in twenty-five years.

The ministry of education determines the allowed enrollments in various schools and departments. Hence, the evolution of educational policy can be seen in the way the ministry has proportioned enrollments to meet the needs of the society and economy over the years. The *proportion* of students in the humanities, agriculture, and law all declined considerably during the past twenty-five years; surprisingly, this has also been the case in the natural sciences. Enrollments in education, social services, engineering, and medical sciences all increased proportionately. Thus, whereas the *number* of students in the humanities, agriculture, law, and the natural sciences increased about fourteenfold, the numbers in the latter categories increased more than forty-three times. The proportion of the total population receiving higher education has risen steadily—from 0.12 percent in 1952 to 1.81 percent in 1976–77. Taiwan has more than enough college graduates to fill its employment requirements.

A friend told me of the four great worries in Taiwan. For parents, the big concern is that their children will do well in school since their entire careers will depend upon this achievement. For teenagers, it is the urgency to pass their exams so they may move up one more step on the educational ladder. For young men, the problem is to find a respectable job in a market that is terribly tight for the well-educated. The biggest problem for young women is to find a suitable husband before the age of twenty-five, when it is beginning to be too late.

The government also has a social-welfare program. The Six-Year Economic-

Development Plan states that "improved social welfare is the ultimate objective of economic development. . . . While economic growth without inflation will be pursued, improvement of social welfare and quality of life will be sought to ensure a balanced socio-economic development." There are two forms of social insurance. The labor-insurance program covers workers in private industry, providing benefits for childbirth, injury, sickness, disability, old age, and death. By the end of 1976 some 1,728,640 workers were covered, but they made up only about half the workers in private industry. The Six-Year Plan calls for intensified inspection to prevent employers (who pay from 70 to 80 percent of the premiums) from underreporting their payrolls. Furthermore, retirement pay is presently awarded in a lump sum rather than in the form of an annuity.

The other main type of insurance is for government employees, who include most teachers. A total of 367,000 such employees had been brought under this plan by the end of 1975. Retirement pay for these workers is also given in one sum. I asked a recently retired professor whether the income from his invested retirement allowance was adequate for his needs, and he readily confessed that it was not. It brings him the equivalent of about a hundred U.S. dollars a month, in addition to a rent-free house (because he is a former faculty member of a leading university) and health insurance. Still, he must earn another two hundred dollars a month for his small household's living expenses. He was one of those who assured me that the standard of living in Taiwan is infinitely higher than it was twenty or even ten years ago, and he is convinced that it is incomparably higher than the standard on the mainland, where so much is rationed and consumer goods are quite costly.

An aim of the government is to eliminate poverty, which is defined by a certain level of income just as it is in the United States. In August 1977, Taiwan Provincial Governor Hsieh Tung-min (later to become vice-president) reported to the Provincial Assembly that four-fifths of the people who had been registered as poor in Taiwan five years before now enjoyed incomes above the poverty line. In 1976 the number of poor families had dropped to 22,144, out of a total population of 86,203 (presumably this does not count cases in the Taipei metropolis). A recent development in rural Taiwan that may lift family incomes is the spread of handicraft industries—the so-called living-room workshops—where components for factory goods are produced by the women of the family (not the old-fashioned handicraft, but probably poorly paid piecework). An American woman who has lived in Taiwan for nearly three years wrote to President Carter about her personal observations. She had seen only one beggar, and that one was not in rags. "No one looks hungry and people of all classes are decently dressed."

BACKGROUND OF TAIWAN'S ECONOMIC DEVELOPMENT

Taiwan's present bustling economic life is partly the result of an American economic-aid program that lasted from 1950 to 1965. At the beginning of the period, the island's economy was characterized by a severely war-damaged infrastructure and minimal manufacturing facilities, shortages of basic necessities, three-digit inflation, a heavy defense burden, and an acute shortage of foreign exchange to finance essential imports. During the next fifteen years the United States injected into Taiwan's economy an average of about one hundred million dollars a year in the form of loans and grants. Most of the aid came as agricultural and industrial supplies and capital goods. Local currency generated by the sale of American commodities reduced inflationary pressures, made up government budget deficits, and financed a number of developmental projects in the areas of agriculture, industry, electric power, transportation, and communications. In addition, the technical-assistance program provided training in the United States for some three thousand Chinese specialists in agriculture, education, industry, and public administration.

By 1965 Taiwan could stand on its own economically, and the aid program was phased out. Thereafter some development was financed by loans from the United States. Loans and loan guarantees committed by the U.S. Export-Import Bank came to $1.6 billion at the end of 1976. These loans were used for expansion programs of the Taiwan Power Company—investments in oil refining, petrochemicals, transportation and communications that contributed to Taiwan's economic-growth potential and stimulated the purchase of American plants and equipment.

The American contribution is only part of the story. Taiwan's spectacular growth is also the result of planning and investment by the government of the Republic of China and the tremendous industry of millions of Chinese entrepreneurs—farmers and fishermen, shopkeepers, traders, bankers, and industrialists—in a largely free-market economy. During the early stages of economic planning, American officials gave a great deal of help. By 1965, when direct American economic aid ended, the Third Four-Year Plan had been completed. Now the planning process is entirely Chinese, though the government hires some foreign experts to check on the installation of equipment procured abroad.

The Economic Planning Council of the Executive Yuan does the macro-planning for a strategy of economic growth, taking into account existing structural weaknesses, the international economic scene and projected develop-

ments, trends in the domestic economy, and the objectives and social policies laid down by the government. The stated purpose of the present Six-Year Plan is "to improve the economic structure, promote economic modernization, and build a society characterized by peace, harmony, happiness, prosperity and justice." The major targets of the plan, which runs from 1975 to 1981, are: higher national income, and improved standards of living and social welfare; controlled population growth, intensified vocational training, and increased employment opportunities; development of slope lands and marine resources, progress toward agricultural mechanization and modernization, and in improved standard of living for farmers and fishermen; stepped-up exploration for energy, development of capital- and technology-intensive industries; completion of the plan for ten major development projects and continued promotion of other infrastructure projects; strengthened trade organizations and active promotion of agriculture, commerce, and industry; and the development of fiscal and monetary policies aimed at an equitable distribution of wealth and continued price stability. Methods for achieving these ambitious and idealistic goals are worked out in great detail, and all branches of the government are involved in executing these national policies. By 1981, Taiwan's gross national product is expected to be 50 percent greater than it was in 1975, and per-capita income is expected to grow to U.S. $1,400 (compared with $706 in 1975). Yet the international scene presents many uncertainties, so the plan is adjusted each year.

The people's livelihood is highly dependent upon foreign trade, and the growth of this trade has been spectacular. In 1952 the value of total exports and imports was only U.S. $303 million. Trade gradually increased until 1965, when it crossed the $1 billion mark. Since then Taiwan's foreign trade has boomed, reaching a value of more than $8 billion in 1973 and more than $15.5 billion in 1976. In only five of the past twenty-five years has the value of exports exceeded the cost of imports.

There has been a great change in the composition of Taiwan's trade abroad. In 1952 only 8 percent of its exports (by value) were industrial products; the rest were derived from agriculture. In 1976 the situation was reversed: industrial products made up 88 percent of the value of exports and agricultural products only 12 percent. Taiwan imports large amounts of oil, machinery and tools, electronics, chemicals, basic metals, and such agricultural products as wheat, corn, soybeans, and raw cotton. Since it is so dependent upon foreign trade for the livelihood of its people, the nation is vulnerable to changes in foreign markets or uncontrollable rises in the prices of the goods it must import to operate the economy. The oil crisis of 1973–74 was a real one for Taiwan.

In 1954, I talked with Mr. K. P. Ch'en, a prominent banker no longer living, who described for me the difficulties in getting overseas Chinese businessmen to invest in Taiwan. The main obstacles were government policy and the attitudes of officials, "who speak a different language" from businessmen, Mr. Ch'en observed. When businessmen asked for guarantees that they could take their profits out of the country, the officials responded, "You are not patriotic." Furthermore, at that time Taiwan had few institutions for the conduct of modern business, very little local capital, no stock market, and a government ban on new private commercial banks. The main problem was the government's obsession with retaking the mainland, which determined tax policy and many other matters vital to business, Mr. Ch'en told me. He hoped the government would adopt more effective policies so that overseas Chinese would develop more confidence in Taiwan and begin to invest there.

This is exactly what happened. In 1954, overseas Chinese invested only U.S. $128,000 in Taiwan. In the following few years, as the climate for investment improved, the figure began to climb into the millions, and by 1976 overseas Chinese had invested U.S. $450 million in a variety of manufacturing enterprises and speculative building projects. By 1976 other foreign investment, mostly American and Japanese, had reached about $1 billion. This is only a small part of total investment in Taiwan, however. The current Six-Year Plan calls for U.S. $35.6 billion in fixed capital investment, of which a little more than half is expected to come from private sources and the rest from the government. Whether such ambitious targets can be met will depend greatly upon the international situation, or more precisely upon American action with respect to Taiwan's security.

A part of this investment figure is a sum equivalent to U.S. $6.5 billion that has been committed to the ten major development projects already underway. A new and an expanded thermal electrical generating plant and two nuclear power plants will enormously increase Taiwan's capacity for electricity. The main railway from Keelung to Kaohsiung is being electrified, and a new railway line is under construction in extremely difficult mountain terrain that will link the present east-coast line with the main line in the west. An up-to-date and beautiful superhighway from the northern to the southern ends of the island is nearly completed and already in use. A new international airport twenty-five miles southwest of Taipei should be opened for traffic in December 1978. Two new harbors are being constructed, one on the central west coast and one on the northeast, that are designed to relieve some of the traffic burden on the present main harbors and to contribute to the development of the regions served by the new facilities.

These are all government-financed contributions to the economic infra-structure. In addition, three important joint government and private projects are the vast petrochemical complex, the new integrated steel mill, and the new shipyard of the China Shipbuilding Corporation, all currently in production near Kaohsiung; these utilize both Chinese and foreign capital. When I visited Taiwan in December 1973, the shipyard was no more than surveyors' marks on an open area near Kaohsiung harbor; in June 1976 I saw a giant tanker under construction there; and by July 1977 that 450,000-ton tanker was under-going its sea trials. The shipyard also includes the world's second-largest dockyard.

Tourism is booming. More than a million visitors came to Taiwan in 1976, with Japanese accounting for nearly half the total. Some parts of Taipei have the appearance of a little Ginza, and good Japanese restaurants abound. Over-seas Chinese, mostly from Hong Kong, are the next-largest group of visitors, and Americans (some 140,000 of them) rank third. The "beautiful island" has spectacular mountain scenery, a lush and manicured countryside, excellent hotels, marvelous Chinese cuisine, and fine shopping facilities. The National Palace Museum, which houses some of the world's greatest collection of Chi-nese art, has drawn more than ten million visitors during the past eleven years.

Tourists spent some U.S. $466 million in Taiwan during 1976. The govern-ment does everything possible to encourage the ever-growing tide of tourists who provide this important source of income. With rising prosperity, more and more inhabitants are able to enjoy Taiwan's scenic spots and recreational facilities. Trains and buses are so crowded it has become difficult to buy a ticket or to make a hotel reservation unless one does so well in advance.

A prime goal of economic planning is to improve the standard of living of the rural population, farmers and fishermen. Although the total land area under cultivation has increased by only 5 percent in the past twenty-five years, agricultural production has more than doubled. Livestock has increased five-fold, and the product of fisheries is seven times what it was a quarter of a century ago. One underlying factor is incentive. As a result of the nonviolent land reform undertaken by the government in the 1950s, 82 percent of the farmers now operate their own land, 9 percent are part-owners, and 9 percent are tenants. In 1952, only 38 percent were owners, 26 percent part-owners, and 36 percent tenants.

Another basic factor is organization. Most of Taiwan's 870,000 farm fami-lies are members of self-governing farmers' associations, which provide banking and credit facilities, do joint marketing of grain and other farm products, purchase fertilizer and pesticides under cooperative arrangements, rent power

tools to the members, and provide livestock insurance. Most important of all, the associations are agencies that transmit scientific information on farming to their members. A Fruit Marketing Cooperative with a membership of nearly ninety-five thousand households works to increase the farmers' share of earnings from the export of fruits, and sixteen self-governing irrigation associations with a membership of more than nine hundred thousand households regulate water use, maintain existing irrigation facilities, and cooperate with the government in implementing new projects.

The Chinese-American Joint Commission on Rural Reconstruction (JCRR) has achieved one of the world's great successes in promoting agricultural modernization in a developing country. Organized in 1948 and operating in Taiwan for more than a quarter of a century, it has pioneered and guided virtually every phase of Taiwan's agricultural improvement. The staff numbers only about 250, but most of the technical personnel and all the Chinese commissioners have studied in American colleges and universities. The JCRR has been dedicated since its beginning to helping rural people to help themselves. Its role is that of a catalyst. It funds development projects undertaken by such public and private agencies as agricultural-experiment stations, farmers' and fishermen's associations, research institutes, agricultural colleges, and a variety of local governmental agencies. The technical divisions of the JCRR carefully study all proposals before approving and funding them, and they exercise close supervision over their implementation. By funding end-user agencies directly, the commission seeks to avoid bureaucratic control and red tape.

Innovations in agriculture conducted with the JCRR's technical and financial assistance include improvements in plant varieties, cultural techniques, and cropping patterns, in irrigation and the application of fertilizers and pesticides, and in the use of slope lands through soil-conservation measures; better methods of breeding cattle, hogs, and poultry and of feeding them and controlling their diseases; and more effective orchard management and efforts to develop the island's forestry industry. The JCRR has also assisted in the improvement of fishing gear, the construction and motorization of deep-sea fishing craft, and the development of better culture techniques in fisheries. In short, the JCRR has brought science and technology to Taiwan's agriculture, fishing, and forestry.

Taiwan has hogs as wonderful as any in the world. Some six million are born each year. Its mushrooms have captured 80 percent of the world export market, and its fruits are world famous. More than sixty million chickens and twenty million ducks were slaughtered in Taiwan in 1976. I visited the Pig Research Institute near Hsinchu, a subsidiary of the Taiwan Sugar Monopoly.

It computerizes the records of its thirty thousand pigs in terms of genetic background, feed, weight, and many other details; I was told that it is the only such computerized pig farm in the world. The institute not only breeds superior strains, it also sells semen to improve the island-wide hog stock.

In its excellent chemical and biological laboratories, the Food Research Institute near Taoyuan studies technical problems connected with food packaging for export and domestic use. It also conducts seminars for home-economics teachers on sanitary handling and storage of foods. Many such organizations, partly staffed with Western-trained Chinese scientists, are assisted by the JCRR in their innovative work.

In spite of all that has been done in the past twenty-five years to increase the volume and improve the quality of agricultural output, there are still serious problems in the rural sector. The average size of the family farm has gradually declined as a result of the system of multiple inheritance. The small size of the average farm—today just over two-and-a-half acres—impedes mechanization just when it is needed most because of increasing labor shortages in agriculture. Farmers' incomes have not kept pace with those in other sectors of the work force, although in absolute terms farmers presently earn much more than they did twenty-five years ago. The government encourages land consolidation and joint farming to achieve economies of scale, while still maintaining private land ownership. Guaranteed prices for feed crops and a system of contracts between farmers and large-scale purchasers for some agricultural products—asparagus and mushrooms, for example—help to stabilize both output and income. Government-guaranteed rice prices that were above the market level resulted in an increase in rice production of nearly 9 percent and enhanced the producers' income in 1976. Prices of fertilizer, a government monopoly, have been progressively reduced, and the government has abolished the compulsory barter system of rice for fertilizer, which discriminated against the farmer.

Government banks have improved agricultural credit facilities and lowered interest rates on loans to farmers for capital improvements. At a farmers' association I visited in 1961, the annual interest rate on loans was 17 percent; at one I visited in 1977, the lending rate was 10.75 percent for guaranteed loans and 11.5 percent for loans without guarantees.

Higher incomes for farmers have made it possible for many of them to enjoy new amenities. Today, 70 percent of farm families own television sets, 75 percent own sewing machines, and 30 percent have refrigerators.

The government also has plans for rural community development, though it lacks the funds to do much at present. (The ROC always faces a choice, of

course, between socially beneficial projects and expenditures for defense. Taiwan's future is insecure, and the ministry of defense is clamoring for a greater share of the national budget.) I was shown a reconstructed village near Taoyuan, with no pretense that it was anything but a model. The homes were almost entirely new cement-and-brick structures with adequate sanitary facilities, there were a few tidy shops—poor by city standards—selling daily necessities, the temple had been renovated in a gaudy style, and there was a recreation center and a new stage for theatricals. I also spent a few hours in an unreconstructed village not far away, with narrow, rutted streets, open sewers, disorderly shops, a few bedraggled and dust-covered trees, and ramshackle houses. Rural Taiwan, as American anthropologists well know, lags far behind the rapidly developing urban sector. There is little reason to doubt, however, that President Chiang Ching-kuo and other government leaders are serious in their intention to reduce the income gap between farmers and city workers and to provide better standards of health and education for the rural population. There is a long road ahead.

POLITICS IN THE REPUBLIC OF CHINA: DEMOCRACY OR POLICE STATE?

Detractors allege that political rule over the Taiwanese populace is held by Mainland oligarchs who wield power through pervasive controls and the suppression of fundamental human freedoms. I consider this description distorted: political realities are much more complex.

The issue of relations between the native Taiwanese population and the million-or-so Mainlanders who arrived after 1945 to replace the Japanese overlords has been extensively discussed. Two decades ago, relations were very strained, but time seems to be gradually diminishing the problem. In 1977 there were some 2.25 million "Mainlanders" among the 14.25 million Taiwanese. Probably a majority of all Mainlanders were born on the island: only their parents' generation has known the other China personally, and that generation is gradually passing from the stage.

The Taiwanese have no real attachment to the Mainland. The memory of the bloody repression of the Taiwanese who revolted against the carpetbagging rule of Nationalist officials more than thirty years ago (in February 1947) may now be fading. For a generation now, Taiwanese children have been receiving the same education as Mainlander children, and the groups are intermixed in the same classes. Still, in most rural areas the language of daily use is still

Fukienese or Hakka, and in large sections of the cities these are the languages of home life and commerce. Most people can speak *kuo-yü*, the language of education, however, and most television programs are in this official language. Nevertheless, Taiwanese intellectuals are uneasy: there seems to be a longing among them to develop a culture of their own.

In 1954 I was told by the president of National Taiwan University (Taita) that Taiwanese made up a little more than half of the student body (4,580, of whom only 760 were women). The members of that educated group are now in their mid-forties. Taita now has about 13,000 students, about half of whom are women. Higher education is equally available to all who can pass the gruelling entrance examinations, but Taiwanese who are graduates of rural and small-town high schools are at a disadvantage. Nevertheless, there are many bright Taiwanese students in the colleges and universities. Intermarriage among college-educated youths is not as unusual as it was a decade or more ago. Mainlander children are moving into businesses owned by Taiwanese, and Mainlander girls are finding jobs that were once the monopoly of native girls. Several well-informed Mainlanders told me they thought the privileged position of their group, particularly of young men, is slipping.

It is safe to say that political power in Taiwan is firmly lodged within the executive branch of the national government. The national legislature is not a countervailing power. Most of the legislators were elected on the Mainland three decades ago and thus have no constituencies. Replacements have been chosen to fill their thinning ranks, and beginning in 1969, supplemental elections have been held for representatives from Taiwan Province. The legislature debates and passes national laws and approves the budget, but laws are so broadly drawn that executive officials have wide scope for interpretation. The court system is theoretically independent, but martial law has been in effect since 1948: it permits secret military trials of defendants who are deemed threatening to the state. Likewise, the legal profession has not been able to establish the independent position it enjoys in the West.

Yet many able officials run a planned economy with great intelligence and try to maintain a stable society with a contented populace. This kind of rule is in the Chinese autocratic tradition, which can change only slowly. One element of that tradition is an examination system for selecting and promoting officials. A member of the Examination Yuan, an old friend, described for me an examination that was being conducted in the summer of 1977 for selection and promotion of officials at various levels of the bureaucracy. After preliminary screening, seventy thousand persons sat for examinations. To ensure fairness, the exam questions were drawn up in secret and the graders worked

in isolation until the process had been completed. My friend had the responsibility of recruiting a committee of thirty-three respected jurists to write the questions pertaining to law and then to read sections of the fifty thousand papers that answered them. He led me to believe that the old system is conducted honestly.

During the past twenty-five years the Republic of China has developed a regular pattern of elections for provincial, municipal, county, and village officials in the territories it controls. Most of the successful candidates are those backed by the ruling party, the Kuomintang. Its Organization Bureau, which has always been headed by a Mainlander, employs a careful screening process to select the candidates deemed suitable to run for office with the backing of the only party whose endorsement really counts. Two other parties merely provide window dressing. China has no tradition of, and little experience in, political pluralism. Yet in November 1977, the election for mayors and magistrates and for the provincial assembly produced surprising results. Independent candidates won a fifth of the races for mayor or magistrate, breaking the Kuomintang's monopoly on these local positions, in addition to twenty-one of the seventy-seven seats in the Provincial Assembly, where only eight independents had previously sat. The elections appeared to be the fairest yet conducted in Taiwan, despite the fact that China's political culture has few supports for democracy as it is understood in the West.

Native Taiwanese are enjoying increasing representation at all levels of government save the very top. A few have achieved cabinet positions by appointment. The appointed governor of the province of Taiwan and the mayor of Taipei were born in Taiwan, and elected provincial assemblymen as well as officials at the local level are overwhelmingly of Taiwanese origin. The cynical may regard this as co-optation, but it seems clearly to be the policy of the new president and his advisers to bring increasing numbers of capable Taiwanese into administrative positions. The new vice-president is Taiwanese.

Rural and small-town governments manage the multitude of local problems and keep the society functioning smoothly. A Taiwanese small-town mayor confessed to me that most of his time is spent in arbitrating disputes. Locally elected officials have only limited powers, however, since taxation is centrally controlled and revenues are allocated at the top. The populace has virtually no say in how its tax dollars will be spent. This may be good for efficiency in a planned economy, but it is poor education for democracy.

Taiwan enjoys freedom of religion, and there is no policy of disparagement or harassment except in cases where religious groups engage in politics. The government publicizes the diversity of sects and doctrines on the island:

Buddhist, Taoist, Christian, Moslem ones, in addition to several local sects. Buddhism has millions of adherents in Taiwan; it is the popular religion among the native folk, helping and consoling them through life's crises. According to government publicity, there are more than twenty-five hundred Buddhist temples attended by nearly seventy-five hundred monks and nuns. Taoism is reportedly represented by nearly two thousand temples, and hundreds of temples are dedicated to local deities such as Ma Tsu (Lady Guardian of the Sea) who are not directly connected with either Buddhism or Taoism, but these are not showplace temples of the sort one may see on the mainland. Shamanism, too, has many believers.

According to the government, there are some 3,000 Protestant churches in Taiwan with more than 500,000 members. There are 12 theological seminaries under Protestant auspices, 13 Bible schools, 9 hospitals, 37 clinics, 2 universities, 4 colleges, 9 high schools, and 350 primary schools and kindergartens. Catholics operate 26 hospitals, 96 dispensaries, 326 primary schools and kindergartens, 26 high schools, 13 technical schools, 3 colleges, 1 university, and 8 seminaries. Catholic communicants number nearly 300,000. Protestant evangelical sects are extremely active. Christian student organizations conduct evangelistic campaigns on many college campuses, and during summer holidays student retreats and conferences are held throughout the island. This is a striking contrast to the suppression of Christianity on the mainland. Bibles printed in Romanized script of Fukienese dialect are prohibited in Taiwan.

The unquenchable paternalism of Chinese officials is obvious from their arrangements for Ghost Festival Day, on August 29, 1977, the fifteenth day of the seventh moon in the lunar calendar. The Taichung city government announced "improvement measures" for the upcoming festival. It designated one temple in each district for the rituals, ordered sacrificial objects to be limited to incense, fruit, and flowers, and decreed that only "proper contests" helpful to physical and mental health would be allowed. People were not to entertain guests, and parades to welcome deities were prohibited. Open-air dramatic performances had to be approved by the authorities and all shows were to be staged for one day only. Microphones were not allowed during performances or at sutra-reading ceremonies. It seems safe to assume that such orders were simply disregarded by the joyous Taiwanese during the festival.

Aside from religion, what is the state of the other fundamental freedoms and rights in the ROC: the right to due process and a speedy trial; the right of free assembly, especially in labor unions; and the freedoms of the press, of speech, and of thought?

Mr. Burton Levin, then director of the Office of the Republic of China in

the Department of State, who was responsible for being informed on such matters, testified on June 14, 1977, before a subcommittee of the House International Relations Committee on human rights in Taiwan. Up to and during the early 1950s, he remarked, the government in Taiwan was obsessed with the fear of communist subversion; there was an atmosphere of fear and repression, with many of the trappings of a police state. In the intervening quarter of a century, Taiwan has evolved toward a more open society. "The police state atmosphere no longer exists, and the average Chinese goes about his daily life without fear of repression." Mr. Levin also cited reasons for the lack of greater progress. First, despite its Western features, Taiwan remains a Chinese society; its political dynamics reflect a highly centralized and personalized Chinese pattern of leadership. In making its compromises between social order and individual rights, Taiwan has predictably given preference to the traditional emphasis on social order and harmony. Second, the Republic of China regards itself as being in a continuing civil war with the People's Republic of China. The government believes that the unequal situation of an island pitted against a continent warrants emergency measures that result in limitations on human rights. Finally, some opponents of the present government express their opposition by violence, which strengthens the hand of the hard-liners who are unsympathetic to human rights.

More specifically, Mr. Levin stated his belief, based upon the wide contacts of the American embassy in Taipei, that torture and cruel treatment have become less frequent in recent years, although reports of such activities persist. He accepted the probability that security services have at times used torture, harsh treatment, and psychological pressure, even though these practices are contrary to the declared policy of the government, but did not think they were widespread. In December 1976, the government stated that there were 254 persons in prisons on sedition charges. Amnesty International has the names of about 200. There have been no reports of political executions in recent years, according to the embassy. Martial law gives the government powers to try a variety of crimes in military courts, to limit political assembly, to prohibit strikes, and to censor the press. Information available to the embassy indicated that people suspected of sedition were detained, often incommunicado and sometimes for months, without being formally charged or tried. "However, in contrast with earlier years of ROC rule on Taiwan when some people simply disappeared, it is our impression that in recent years detainees are eventually either charged and tried or released," Mr. Levin said.

This is the grim side of the picture. But the long-term trend, in Mr. Levin's opinion, promises to be toward greater respect for individual liberties. The

government of the Republic of China has become increasingly conscious of human-rights considerations, perhaps particularly as they may affect American relationships with the Republic of China.

In a much harsher critique, Professor James Seymour of New York University, a member of Amnesty International, testified before the same committee that the regime in Taiwan was a police state wherein a minority of Mainlanders represses the human rights of a population made up mainly of Taiwanese. He detailed several notorious cases involving arbitrary imprisonment to suppress opposition views that had nothing to do with communism, harassment of the supporters of opposition politicians, and suppression of magazines that were critical of government policy. He listed a series of laws in addition to martial law that he believed are used to threaten and silence dissidents, and spoke of the "arbitrary, lawless nature of government on Taiwan." He maintained that factories and all other institutions are infiltrated by secret agents, and that any serious labor agitation is quickly repressed. In Professor Seymour's view, the threat to the security of the people on Taiwan "is not some remote enemy, but rather their present, American backed rulers." The Formosan Association for Human Rights, an émigré opposition group in the United States, has painted an even grimmer picture. (I do not accept this hostile view, although I believe that the security apparatus has been excessively harsh in the past and may become so again in the face of renewed adversity.)

The government does not permit strikes. In effect, it acts as the bargaining agent on wages and working conditions. According to government statistics, average monthly wages in most branches of industry rose between 78 and 109 percent in the last three years, staying ahead of the inflation in consumer prices, which rose about 60 percent in the same period. The average income of persons in service occupations, however, lagged behind inflation. Both the government and the Kuomintang work diligently for the support of youth and intellectuals. Hostile attitudes among these three groups—labor, youth, and intellectuals—were an important element in the downfall of the Republic of China on the Mainland, and the leadership does not intend to let that happen again. Hence, a vigilant security system is maintained.

Every fit young male must serve his turn in the armed forces, but middle-school graduates are not "sent down" to the countryside, nor are farmers forced to remain on the farm. Those who wish to travel within Taiwan simply buy their tickets and go. Travel abroad, however, is strictly controlled. Every resident carries an identity card and must register with the police when he moves. In short, the picture is mixed: liberties are restricted by the perceived requirements of security.

Indoctrination is pervasive. School children undergo intensive and continuous training in loyalty to the group, to the nation, and to the national leaders. On any night one may see television shows filled with patriotic themes. One evening in the summer of 1977, for example, all three channels showed exactly the same entertainment that had been staged for delegates and guests at a conference of the Asian People's Anti-Communist League: a Hollywood-style "spectacular" whose main themes were love of the country and dedication to liberating the brothers on the Mainland. This was not unusual.

In the handsome building commemorating Sun Yat-sen, one enters a vast hall and faces a large statue of the father of the country sitting in a sober and contemplative pose, not unlike that of Abraham Lincoln in his memorial in Washington. Sun's memorial hall in Taipei is devoted to inculcating patriotism. In the summer of 1977, one large exhibition space extolled the youthful heroes who struggled to overthrow the Manchu dynasty. Another, commemorating the fortieth anniversary of the July 7 Incident of 1937, showed the long struggle of Chinese against Japan, beginning with efforts of the Taiwanese to evade a Japanese takeover of their province in 1895 and continuing to China's victory in 1945. A special exhibit displayed the Kuomintang's version of the treacherous history of the Chinese Communist movement. It depicted a barbarous regime on the Mainland and the miserable life of the people there. Another hall chronicled the life and achievements of the late President Chiang Kai-shek, and a Hall of Fame showed paintings of some forty Chinese heroes from mythical times almost to the present. One Manchu emperor made the list because of his accomplishments in extending China's borders far into Central Asia. An even larger memorial hall for the late president is under construction, and a beautiful shrine in the northern part of Taipei is dedicated to heroes who gave their lives for the country.

The press is obedient, but not because of precensorship. A network of relationships with, and guidance from, the party and government agencies lets every responsible owner or editor know the correct line on most issues. The government has abruptly terminated a few magazines that showed too much independence. Thus, according to a well-informed observer, there is neither complete freedom of the press nor close censorship, but the press is freer than it was even a few years ago.

In August 1977, when Secretary of State Cyrus Vance was about to leave for Peking, the moderator, deputy moderator, and general secretary of the General Assembly of the Presbyterian Church in Taiwan (the largest Protestant denomination) signed a Declaration on Human Rights, which appealed to President Carter to insist on guaranteeing the security, independence, and

freedom of the people on Taiwan while pursuing the normalization of our relationship with Communist China. "In order to achieve our goal of independence and freedom for the people of Taiwan," the declaration added, "we urge our government to face reality and take effective measures whereby Taiwan may become a new and independent country." In the eyes of the authorities, this proposal was virtually *lèse majesté*. They immediately confiscated the August 21 issue of *Taiwan Presbyterian Weekly*, which published the declaration, but they merely questioned the signers.

A friend of mine who dared to publish two scholarly books on the history of the Chinese Communist movement suffered the confiscation of all the copies in Taiwan, though the book is available in libraries in the United States and Japan and has been reprinted in Hong Kong. My friend has found no means of redress, though he was not deprived of his college teaching position there. Most books on the communist movement are issued only for limited circulation by approved agencies.

It is not easy, however, to measure the effects of this pervasive effort to inculcate a sense of national pride and to control what the people learn about conditions on the Mainland. All Chinese seem deeply proud of their nation's past and their unique culture. During the past decade a major effort in Taiwan has been dedicated to a cultural-renaissance movement, the revival of traditional learning, philosophy, art, and the theatre. Yet Western culture has a strong allure for the young. Many television commercials use Western fashion as the basis for their sales pitch. Several well-informed persons have told me that native Taiwanese are not much influenced by the government's propaganda efforts, and that the government is aware of this.

Two surprising experiences may illustrate the government's problem in convincing older Mainlanders of the correct line about conditions across the straits. A taxi driver who was born on the Mainland discovered that one of his riders, a Chinese woman married to an American, was a fellow provincial. He burst into his native dialect and announced that he had brothers who taught school on the Mainland, that he knew conditions were not so bad there, and that he would return immediately if he could. His excited talk was unmistakably spontaneous and forthright. A shopkeeper from the Mainland became very friendly as we examined his wares. There was no one else in the shop. To my surprise he kept saying in different ways that the United States should enter into diplomatic relations with the People's Republic; America should become friendly with the Mainland. He was outspokenly hostile toward the late president, Chiang Kai-shek, and his son, who was then the premier, and

he was outraged by the immoral behavior of "bar girls" near where he lived, with hotels, which he said were simply procurers, and with the need to give "hung-pao" (gifts) to officials. Besides, he wanted to be reunited with his parents on the Mainland. These were two chance encounters with Mainlanders who apparently were not persuaded by the government's propaganda.

A Taiwanese friend told me that a woman writer from the island, now living in Canada, spent many years on the Mainland and became very anticommunist. Her stories, set in the Chinese People's Republic, are popular in Taiwan, but she disclosed facts that contradict the official line about miserable conditions on the Mainland. Her stories are a source of unauthorized information for the discerning.

The social scene in Taiwan appears to be remarkably stable today. If this is really the case, prosperity, at least for most city folk, may be one reason. So long as the economy grows faster than the population, and so long as income distribution is perceived as fair, there may be no cause for serious concern. Crime seems not to be as serious a problem as it is in the United States and Western Europe, though house robberies are not infrequent in Taipei. The Six-Year Economic-Development Plan notes the growth of adolescent crime and proposes remedial measures on an experimental basis. The strong Chinese sense of morality is shared by most of the population, and there is an efficient police force, though it is not devoid of the petty graft found in many cities of the world.

I was struck by the good manners and mild appearance of nearly all the Chinese I saw in Taiwan. Aggressive behavior is not nearly so common there as it is in American cities, particularly New York. The constant inculcation of traditional values and the Chinese practice of raising children very strictly to be obedient, respectful to their superiors, and considerate to others may account for this decorum. Yet a Chinese friend warned me against superficial appearances. People on the street, he said, all seem unconcerned and relaxed, but this is a false front they have been trained to show. Actually there is a great deal of concealed nervousness about the present tense situation, he said, referring to the upcoming trip of Cyrus Vance to Peking in August 1977. My friend was certainly correct about the intense apprehension the Chinese feel about American actions with respect to their country's future. Nearly all my Chinese friends, both Mainlanders and Taiwanese, asked me whether America would desert them. A few speculated on how long their army could hold out if attacked, whether the air force could protect the cities, and how long the navy could keep the sea lanes open.

In considering the complex problem of the development of political life in Taiwan, one must bear in mind China's autocratic and bureaucratic traditions of government, as well as the intellectual and social developments that have occurred over the past century as Western ideas have gradually penetrated the consciousness of Chinese intellectuals. Those who make policy in Taiwan, as well as the general population, are affected by both of these influences. The Taiwanese today are much better educated and far more prosperous than any previous Chinese population. Their longing for greater freedom and personal security and their efforts to achieve greater participation in the decisions that affect their lives cannot but shape the future of Chinese politics. It took Japan a century, a defeat in war, and a period of foreign occupation to reach its present stage of democratic life, and there is no assurance that Taiwan will follow Japan's path toward democracy. The trend seems to be in that direction, but it might be reversed if the island's security became really questionable. A communist takeover would surely reverse the trend.

Any remarks about the future of Taiwan must take the people into account. Whatever the strategic or the international political considerations that argue for American recognition of the People's Republic of China, there is still the important moral question: what of the security and future lives of nearly seventeen million people on Taiwan? This figure includes more than five million children and six hundred thousand elderly people, in addition to fathers and mothers and families, teachers and factory workers, farmers and shop-keepers—a multitude of people like ourselves.

It seems certain that very few inhabitants of the island wish to come under communist rule. Probably they would fight and die for freedom as long as their armaments held out. Subjugation is not their only peril, however. Taiwan's economy is bound up with foreign trade; nearly half its gross national product comes from exports. It is fair to ask whether this commerce could continue on anything like its present scale if the government of the Republic of China lost the recognition of its second most important trading partner, and probably the recognition of smaller nations following the American lead. There is also the probability that the PRC would mount an economic offensive to harass and intimidate Taiwan's trading partners, and possibly a naval blockade to threaten shipping. Either or both could cripple this vital element in the livelihood of Taiwan's people.

One can assume the best—that the PRC will leave Taiwan alone to prosper as a minor Japan—or the worst—that it will do all in its power to bring the island under its rule, no matter what the people there desire. At stake is the future of seventeen million humans.

4 ramon h. myers

a united states policy

For more than a quarter of a century two political regimes have existed, each claiming to represent China. In the famous Shanghai Communiqué, however, the United States acknowledged for the first time that " all Chinese on either side of the Taiwan Strait maintain there is but one China and that Taiwan is a part of China." How the Chinese on either side of the Taiwan Strait continue to define themselves symbolically will be for the Chinese people alone to decide in their own time: no outside power can do it for them.

Yet the United States obviously wants a peaceful resolution to the problem: the use of force by one regime to impose its will on the other would seriously undermine U.S. interests. Since these regimes have developed so differently from each other, a resolution through force would also mean that human rights on either side of the Taiwan Strait would be threatened or violated. Therefore, the informal stable balance of power that has long existed between the two regimes must be maintained if the process of modernization is to continue in each and if political power is to be transferred gradually to new leaders. These are conditions that would lead to a negotiated settlement, and the United States can and ought to cultivate them.

The states of East Asia are now vitally concerned with nation building, an undertaking that requires peace and stability. International events that promote political instability and create economic uncertainty, such as new agreements or alliances between states that threaten the existing balance of power,

disrupt this activity and threaten the interests of all East Asian countries and the United States. For example, a continuing stable balance of power between the PRC and the ROC in their relationships with the United States not only benefits East Asia but also helps to maintain a standoff between the Soviet Union and the United States.

The linchpin in this arrangement, then, is the security and sovereignty of the two regimes that are in competition to represent China. Here lies the great challenge to the United States, which must use its diplomatic skills to ensure the continued existence of these two independent regimes and at the same time develop bilateral relationships with both that will benefit all of the concerned parties politically and economically. In the first four sections of this essay I will discuss the new conditions in East Asia and at home that justify a United States policy toward East Asia based upon the "equilibrium strategy." In the final section I will outline the procedures by which this strategy can be translated into action.

FUTURE TRENDS IN EAST ASIA

If revolution, war, and civil war characterized the second quarter of the twentieth century in East Asia, the final decades of this century should be known as a time of nation building. In the late 1970s a more pragmatic leadership in the PRC is attempting to consolidate power and develop a powerful, modern state by the end of the century. To that end the new leaders are reforming the educational system and reorganizing their economy. Meanwhile, other East Asian states have been trying for some time to maintain their political stability and achieve rapid economic development.

There are two major difficulties with which these states must contend. First, they must somehow accommodate the great increases in population that are expected. Each must expand employment to cover a growing work force of young people, integrate a large stratum of educated youth with the older, conservative sector of society, and provide the higher living standards more people have come to expect. Despite recent projections that the world population growth rate is slowing down, the situation is still ominous. The East Asian population is expected to expand from 1,012 million in 1975 to 1,660 million in 2000.[1] Except for Japan, each country in the region now has a very high proportion of people under sixteen years of age who are consuming much and producing little. By the year 2000 improved health standards and increased

---

[1] United Nations Department of Economic and Social Affairs, *World Population Prospects As Assessed in 1973* (New York: United Nations, 1977), table 28.

longevity will produce an expanding proportion of elderly who will also have to be supported.

A second problem ticks away like a time bomb. Most East Asian states have "strong-men" rule, and before the turn of the century a transfer of political power must take place from aging strong men and their supporters to new leaders. Will the transfer be smooth or rocky? In these autocratic states the pivotal leaders are already advanced in age. Presidents Park Chung-hee and Kim Il-sung in South and North Korea are both in their sixties; the top leaders in the PRC, aside from Hua Kuo-feng, are in their seventies; Premier Chiang Ching-kuo and his new vice-president Hsieh Tung-min in the ROC are sixty-eight and seventy-two.

In such regimes power usually passes to slightly younger men of the same generation, but even so the transfer involves more than a simple musical-chairs rotation of aging leaders. The new leaders inherit the problems of legitimizing their rule, securing their bases of power to ensure their continued ability to exercise authority, and coordinating different interest groups in order to moderate their demands. Future leaders will probably come from the bureaucracy or the military since current opposition groups are either nonexistent or too weak to demonstrate strong dissent. These new leaders will probably want to continue present efforts to achieve rapid modernization and economic development provided their energies are not dissipated in a struggle to maintain political power, but a shaky transfer of leadership could produce such confusion and instability that political and economic decay would result.

If these predictions are valid, then East Asian strongmen may be devoting most of their time and energy to internal affairs; they will take seriously only those international matters that appear to have serious implications for domestic stability and tranquility. How then should the power and influence of the United States be used in East Asia until the turn of the century and beyond? What are the vital interests of the United States in an East Asia that is experiencing both modernization and more painful social and political adjustments?

THE BALANCE OF POWER IN EAST ASIA

A major power like the United States can pursue its interests only if peace and security exist throughout the globe. Some great powers, naturally, prefer unrest and turmoil because these conditions best serve their expansionist intentions. In East Asia peace and security depend upon long-standing, delicately contrived power balances among states, most of which have evolved since

World War II. Some of these originated from negotiated agreements, others from stalemates.

In serious disagreements among political regimes over national boundaries, the sharing of international resources such as the sea, ideology, and so on, a balance of power exists when each side perceives that any aggressive action toward the other will prove more costly than beneficial. What are the current power-balance arrangements in East Asia?

Japan and the Soviet Union maintain such a balance: these superpowers still have not negotiated a peace treaty to conclude World War II, yet they have negotiated bilateral agreements on fishing rights in Northwest Pacific waters. The Soviet Union worries that Japan may deepen its relationship with the PRC. Recent Japanese moves toward closer economic and political ties with China, reflected in a recent U.S. $20 billion trade agreement between the two countries and negotiated on a formal peace treaty, have resulted in cooler Japanese-Soviet relations.[2] The Soviet Union would be deeply suspicious of Japanese intentions should that country begin to develop a military strike force. Japan, in turn, is bitter over the Soviet refusal to negotiate a settlement of the Northern Territories issue. It is also suspicious of Soviet intentions in Northeast Asia. Nevertheless, both sides continue to confer and negotiate issues separately in the hope of achieving their own objectives.

North and South Korea maintain a very delicate balance of power—one of the most sensitive arrangements in East Asia. South Korea's economy and its per-capita gross national product (GNP) are growing far faster than North Korea's, however, and the impact of North Korea's serious foreign-debt problem will fall heavily upon its economy in the next few years. Unless a major global recession occurs, or protectionism becomes more widespread in the developed world—a development that might adversely influence the volume of exports from South Korea—the gap between South and North Korea will widen. Each side struggles to modernize its military and to replace retiring personnel, and each strives to gain the economic power to enable it to wage a contest for ultimate unification of the Korean Peninsula.

The balance of power between the Soviet Union and the PRC is also a

---

[2] See Craig R. Whitney, "Moscow's Relations with Tokyo Cooling," the *New York Times*, April 10, 1978. In recent months a major defense debate has erupted in Japan. One thrust in this debate so far has come from Mr. Shin Kanemaru, director general of Japan's Defense Agency, a position that is roughly equivalent to the secretary of defense. Mr. Kanemaru was quoted in mid-May as saying "Russian warships and other vessels make such frequent appearances in the Sea of Japan these days that we might as well refer to those waters as the Sea of Russ." See Henry Scott-Stokes, "Defense Increases Urged by Japanese," the *New York Times*, Sunday, May 14, 1978.

delicate one. Disagreement on territorial boundaries is still serious, and strong ideological differences persist. Each side has strengthened its military posture toward the other. In early April 1978, Brezhnev is reported to have called for strengthened defenses against China, a pronouncement designed as much to "sustain military morale in an isolated region where duty is cold and bleak" as to warn the PRC not to alter the balance of power between the two states.[3] The PRC has continually tried to convince other nations, especially the United States, to offer a more vigorous opposition to Soviet expansionism. For example, it urged President Carter to develop the neutron bomb. The Soviet Union remains apprehensive about any new alliances the PRC might conclude with other major powers.

The PRC and the ROC also have established a balance of power with each other. Neither side has been able to develop a strike force capable of destroying the military power of the other, and each fully realizes that only internal turmoil in the rival country will give it a chance to overturn the political system of its opponent.

Each of these balance-of-power arrangements has profound implications for the others. For example, if the United States were suddenly to sever its relations with the ROC in order to achieve full diplomatic ties with the PRC, the Soviet Union might fear that the balance of power between itself and the PRC as well as between the ROC and PRC had shifted in a way that threatened its military security. The USSR might also perceive a new U.S.-PRC alignment as a threat. The Soviet response would then be unpredictable. Retaliatory action might range from strengthening its military forces and speeding up the arms race to seeking new alliances with other regimes, such as the ROC, to offset the shift in the East Asian power balance.

Such conjectures are, of course, highly speculative, but they should not be taken lightly. The leaders of East Asian states consider stable power balances necessary for their foreign policy. Thus, should not preservation of a stable balance among East Asian states be a basic cornerstone of American foreign policy in the Far East? If not, how will the United States react if one of these states suddenly disturbs the balance of power? Will this not create new uncertainties for us? In similar fashion, other states will perceive any precipitous acts by the United States that alter an existing balance of power—for example, abandonment of the ROC in order to normalize relations with the PRC—as threats to their self-interest. The United States has a major stake in maintain-

---

[3] Daniel Southerland, "Why Brezhnev Lashes Out at US, China," *Christian Science Monitor*, April 10, 1978.

ing the delicate power balances that now exist in East Asia, particularly in view of the American public's new mood of caution regarding use of U.S. resources, as well as its resolve to protect long-standing American special interests in East Asia.

AMERICAN PUBLIC OPINION AND AMERICAN INTERESTS IN EAST ASIA

After the military withdrawal of the United States from Southeast Asia in the mid-1970s, public opinion at home naturally changed. The former hope that American power could shape another country's destiny was replaced by a new mood. Most Americans believed that their nation's resources should be utilized at home to deal with the energy crisis, improve the material living standards and rights of minorities and women, and solve the problems of high unemployment and inflation. Instead of spending American resources abroad, America should husband its resources to solve domestic problems. This mood of isolationism has spread widely. How long it will last is not certain, but both the public and its leaders now recognize new national priorities for the next decade.

Many Americans also believe that the United States should establish full-scale diplomatic relations with the PRC but retain its existing relations with the ROC. Periodic public-opinion surveys "confirm the inability of public pro-normalization sentiment to overcome the hurdle of abandoning Taiwan."[4] In other words, a majority of Americans believe that it is in the best interest of their country to establish normal ties with the PRC, but a similar majority do not want the United States to abandon the ROC. How can public opinion be translated into a workable China policy for the United States? Before answering this question, let us first examine briefly American interests in East Asia and then consider the nature of the two political regimes that for over a quarter of a century have claimed to represent China.

As Norma Schroder noted earlier, the United States has a vital stake in East Asia through its foreign trade and investments. Any sudden threat to these investments and markets might cause more unemployment at home. Any deterioration in American foreign trade and investment in East Asia would also cause the flight of capital from Taiwan and a loss of business confidence, and weaken prospects for economic development there. U.S. economic inter-

---

[4] Kevin P. Phillips, "US Opinion on Taiwan," *Baltimore News American*, February 14, 1978.

ests in East Asia are best served by policies that promote more trade within this region, increase American direct investments there, and make advanced technology available to East Asian industry and agriculture alike. If the United States also guarantees to East Asian businessmen sales in its high per-capita-income markets, the prospects for expanded trade between East Asia and ourselves will be bright.

Another vital American interest in East Asia is simply the exchange of people and ideas. Many East Asian students have already been educated and received professional training in the United States. Some of them have returned home and influenced their colleagues and organizations in complex ways that will hasten the process of modernization, and more will do so in the future. Expanding the exchange of peoples and ideas through travel and education can only improve communication and understanding between ourselves and those East Asian countries that are undergoing rapid social and economic modernization.

The spread of totalitarian rule over the Eurasian continent since 1945 is now a historical reality. It is common knowledge that those political systems prefer to stifle the free movement and exchange of people, ideas, goods, and capital. Nevertheless, the more the East Asian states on the periphery of the Asian mainland can be helped to evolve toward freer, more pluralistic political and economic systems, the greater the possibility that U.S. interests in that region can be promoted and realized.

It is within this broad context, then, that the problem of the two China regimes must be examined. On the one hand, the likelihood remains great that all East Asian states will be preoccupied with domestic issues in the years to come. On the other hand, since 1945 a number of delicate but stable balance-of-power relationships among East Asian states have evolved that have made it possible for all parties to pursue their self-interests peacefully. The United States needs peace and stability in this region for its many economic relationships to continue to bear fruit. In such an environment, the variety of exchange relations the United States presently maintains with East Asian states (except North Korea, of course) is bound to increase. With this background, let us now examine closely the nature of the two China regimes.

THE TWO CHINA REGIMES

First, these two regimes should be put into historical perspective. Few Americans are aware that although both the Chinese states insist on the ideal

of one China, Taiwan and the Pescadores have never been more than an out-lying region of the Chinese heartland. The term "China" (*Chung-kuo*) itself came into use before the birth of Christ, but it only referred to the various states in the central Yellow River valley. This term gradually came to denote all of Mainland China, but Taiwan, like Outer Mongolia, was not brought under the sway of a mainland regime until the late seventeenth century. Moreover, the innovative impulse to bring about this political extension did not come from the Chinese themselves but from their Manchu conquerors, although Chinese settlers from Fukien and Kwangtung provinces had brought Taiwan and the Pescadores well within the Chinese cultural arena by the late eight-eenth century.

Peking's current irredentist claims regarding Taiwan and the Pescadores have some emotional and moral force, but they are not totally convincing. Mao Tse-tung, at least in the 1930s, also advanced irredentist claims regarding Outer Mongolia, but these have been mostly forgotten without serious damage to the Chinese national psyche. Similarly, the ties between the territories of Taiwan and the Pescadores and the Chinese polity on the mainland are weak. The feelings of the Mainlanders today about Taiwan, for instance, certainly are not comparable to the powerful Chinese outcry in 1919 for the return of Shantung (Confucius's birthplace) from Japanese imperial control. The songs and slogans urging the liberation of Taiwan that visitors to the PRC hear or read echo the sentiments of the leaders rather than those of the common people. Even though the post-Mao leadership has inserted in the preamble to the March 5, 1978, constitution (the third constitution published since 1949) a statement that Taiwan will be liberated, this can be interpreted simply as a means of rallying factions and legitimizing the new leadership before another power group tries to use the same slogan to advance its cause.[5] Furthermore, Peking's shrill demand that Taiwan be "restored to the motherland" must be balanced against the PRC's *realpolitik* interest in a strong American presence in the Far East to counter Soviet expansionist tendencies.[6]

Although Taiwan was part of a single Chinese state for about two hundred years, complex international developments since 1895 have gradually given that island the character of a sovereign state. Until 1885, of course, the Ch'ing court made Taiwan and the Pescadores a prefecture of Fukien province; only

---

[5] See "Constitution of People's Republic of China," *Hsinhua Weekly*, no. 10 (March 11, 1978), p. 49.
[6] This seems particularly valid in the light of a recent Sino-Soviet border incident in early May 1978. See "Peking Accuses Soviet Forces of a Raid on Manchurian Border," the *New York Times*, May 12, 1978.

after 1885 did they become a province. On April 17, 1895, however, Japan acquired the islands as part of the Treaty of Shimonoseki concluding the first Sino-Japanese war. On November 26, 1943, leaders of Great Britain, the United States, and China convened at the Cairo Conference and declared that "all the territories Japan has stolen from the Chinese, such as Manchuria, Formosa, and the Pescadores, shall be returned to the Republic of China."[7] Later, on July 26, 1945, the Potsdam Proclamation reaffirmed the Cairo Conference declaration by stating that "the terms of the Cairo Conference shall be carried out." And so they were on October 26, 1945, when the Office of the Taiwan Administrator, an agency of the Republic of China, announced that the island of Taiwan had again become a province of China.[8] With the inauguration of the People's Republic of China by the Chinese Communist Party on October 1, 1949, a new political regime was established on the Asian mainland. In December of that same year, the government of the Republic of China moved its "temporary" capital from Canton to Taipei in order to perpetuate that political regime. Since that year the two China regimes have been a reality.

Further developments strengthened the international legitimacy of these two political regimes. In June 1951, John Foster Dulles worked out an arrangement whereby neither the delegates from the ROC nor those from the PRC were invited to the conference concluding a Japanese Peace Treaty. Instead, Japan had to conclude separate bilateral peace treaties with the ROC and the PRC, even though both regimes publicly objected to this course of settlement. On September 8, 1951, the Allied Powers and Japan signed the Japanese Peace Treaty at San Francisco. Article 2 of the treaty stated that "Japan renounces all right, title and claim to Formosa and the Pescadores." On April 28, 1952, the ROC and Japan signed a bilateral peace treaty in which Japan renounced "all right, title and claim to Taiwan and Penghu (Pescadores) as well as the Spratly Islands and the Paracel Islands." It also stated that the "terms of the Treaty shall, in respect of the Republic of China, be applicable to all territories which are now, or which may hereafter be, under the control of its Government."[9] This last statement implied that former Japanese territories on the Mainland might again come under the control of the Republic of China.

On December 2, 1954, the United States and the Republic of China signed a Mutual Defense Treaty. Article 5 of that treaty stated that any armed attack

---

[7] Hungdah Chiu, "China, the United States, and the Question of Taiwan," *China and the Question of Taiwan: Documents and Analysis,* edited by Hungdah Chiu (New York: Praeger, 1973), p. 113.

[8] Ibid., p. 114.

[9] Ibid., p. 127.

in the West Pacific area directed against either the territories of the United States or the ROC would endanger peace and security. Article 6 identified the territories in question as Taiwan and the Pescadores and the island territories in the West Pacific under U.S. jurisdiction.[10]

Since 1971 a number of states have transferred their diplomatic recognition from the ROC to the PRC. Most have done so because of strong pressure from Peking demanding a complete break with the ROC. Admittedly, many of these same states might have maintained their diplomatic ties with the ROC if that regime had not insisted upon claiming to be the sole legitimate government representing China, but Peking undoubtedly would have exerted similar pressures to isolate that regime regardless of the name it gave itself. The combination of the ROC's firm stance and pressure from Peking ultimately forced Japan to break, at least temporarily, with the ROC.

Japan and the PRC signed a nine-article declaration on September 29, 1972, ending the state of war between the two governments. Article 2 of that declaration read: "the Japanese government recognizes the People's Republic of China as the only lawful government of China."[11] Article 3 went on to state that "the People's Republic of China emphatically declares: Taiwan is an inseparable part of the territory of the People's Republic of China. The Japanese government completely understands and is in accord with this position of the Chinese government."[12]

Although Article 3 seemed to abrogate the terms of the bilateral treaty that Japan had signed with the ROC on April 28, 1952, the ROC still survived as a sovereign regime, even in Japan's eyes.[13] Japan, along with many other states, had relegated the ROC government to a kind of international limbo, but after a year or so the two nations established liaison office arrangements to handle relations between them.

The character of the ROC as a sovereign state with jurisdiction only over Taiwan and the Pescadores had already been reinforced by the Mutual

---

[10] Ibid., pp. 250–51 for this document in its entirety.

[11] These articles in the original Chinese can be found in *Jen-min jih-pao* [*People's Daily*], September 30, 1972, p. 1. See also Jerome Alan Cohen and Hungdah Chiu, *People's China and International Law: A Documentary Study* (Princeton: Princeton University Press, 1974), 21611–12. I have used my translation of these articles rather than the one in Cohen and Chiu.

[12] *Jen-min jih-pao*, September 30, 1972, p. 1.

[13] To be sure, in November 1972 Japanese government sources still indicated that Taiwan had not yet been returned to China (the PRC government). See "Tokyo Still Asserts Status of Taiwan Is Not Determined," the *New York Times*, November 6, 1972.

Defense Treaty of 1954 with the United States. The treaty made it clear that the only grounds for U.S. assistance in defense of the ROC was aggression toward these specific territories.

Both the ROC and the PRC have claimed to represent the national entity called "China," and both have used this term to denote territories partly held by the other. Both regimes have also talked of liberating each other's territories. The PRC, however, has been more strident in its claims than the ROC. By the mid-1970s, the ROC was playing down its insistence on reestablishing control of the Mainland, even renouncing the use of force to do so.[14] The PRC, on the other hand, has refused to alter its stance. It continues to declare that it will "brook no interference" by any outside power in the internal Chinese affairs that relate to Taiwan.[15]

On December 8, 1954, PRC foreign minister Chou En-lai criticized the 1954 Mutual Security Treaty by saying it "increased the danger of the extension of the United States aggression against China."[16] He labeled the agreement a "treaty of naked aggression." Later events have proved this charge to be groundless. Far from encouraging the ROC to attack the Mainland, the treaty strongly discouraged such action. ROC leaders, after all, depend upon U.S. military support, and they could not attack the PRC and still be assured of that backing. The leaders of the ROC have gradually come to realize that the United States in effect recognizes the existence of different territories controlled by separate regimes each referring to itself as China, and they have tailored their rhetoric to fit this reality.

---

[14] Numerous examples could be cited, but the most recent is an official statement made by Premier Chiang Ching-kuo on September 23, 1977. It conveyed the argument that "the truth of the China issue" was not the so-called "Taiwan issue"—whether Taiwan should be merged into the present constituency of Mainland China—but the future of China itself—whether it was to be democratic or communist. See *Free China Weekly* 18, no. 3 (September 25, 1977) : 1. This argument could be interpreted as meaning that it was imperative that some sovereign state continue to control Taiwan to ensure rule by a democratic rather than a communist regime.

[15] On October 3, 1977, Ed Cony and Peter R. Kann of the *Wall Street Journal* interviewed Chinese Vice Foreign Minister Yu Chan in Peking. They wrote: "Mr Yu also said that any American statement that the US has vital interests in the peace and stability of the Taiwan region would be unacceptable to China." See "Formulas for Taiwan Accord with US Flatly Rejected by High Official," the *Wall Street Journal*, October 3, 1977, p. 5. See also documents in Cohen and Chiu, *People's China*, 2: 1420–21, 1426, 1610, 1611, and 1628. To be sure, PRC leaders have occasionally stated that they would not use force to liberate Taiwan, but these assertions have been contradicted by other statements suggesting that the PRC can use any means it sees fit to "liberate" Taiwan.

[16] Chiu, "China," p. 147.

THE "EQUILIBRIUM STRATEGY" APPLIED
TO THE CHINA PROBLEM

At present the United States and the PRC conduct a limited exchange of goods and people. More bilateral agreements can expand the flow, but the gap between the present volume of exchange and the amount that could occur under normal diplomatic relations between the two countries is probably minimal, especially since unstable economic conditions within the PRC have greatly influenced trade.

Of course the PRC can always refrain from entering into new agreements because the United States has not met its terms for normalization, but the lessons learned from six years of relations between the two countries suggest unequivocally that it would not do so. That nation's leaders have not said what they will do if their terms are not met.

The two sides agree that normalization of relations on Peking's terms would involve both high costs and substantial benefits; thus they have failed to reach a settlement. How can this impasse be broken? First, the discussions must be shifted from these costs and benefits to other issues of mutual interest. Therefore, why not place a moratorium on all discussion related to normalization and focus instead upon a series of other issues that appear to be more likely to be resolved?

In private discussions, for example, the American side might stress to the PRC leaders that the question of which regime will ultimately represent the Chinese people is for the ROC and PRC leaders alone to resolve, although the American side hopes for a peaceful decision. The United States should also notify the PRC of current efforts within the ROC to give the Taiwanese people a larger share in their government. This reallocation of political power will affect future relations between the ROC and PRC. For example, should the ROC leadership then renounce its historical mission of "returning to the mainland" and advocate a different strategy based upon cultivating friendly relations with the PRC, a dialogue between Peking and Taipei might begin.

The United States also can reassure the PRC leaders that its major goal in East Asia is peace and economic development, including an expanded international exchange of goods and people. Each side has different ideas about how these goals can be achieved and maintained, but the PRC leaders will certainly appreciate steadfast American support of its present commitments in East Asia as long as that support does not upset existing power balances. This statement might appear paradoxical in the light of Peking's current demands for normalization of relations, but the PRC has not been displeased, for example, by a strong American presence in East Asia that checks the Soviet

Union. It has already expressed concern that an American withdrawal from the ROC might invite an undesirable Soviet presence in the southwest Pacific.[17]

More importantly, the 1954 Mutual Security Treaty between the United States and the ROC serves to restrain a preemptive strike by the ROC on the Mainland. The United States should point out to the PRC that the treaty helps to maintain a military balance between the PRC and the ROC by removing the need for the ROC to develop its own nuclear military capabilities, a development that would simply create additional tension in the region.

Of course, there are many other problems the PRC and the United States can consider. First, both sides might try to resolve the long-standing legal disagreements about compensation for American assets in the PRC that have been frozen. Second, issues related to the establishment of trade, financing, and communications between the two countries can be negotiated on a step-by-step basis, possibly ending in the conclusion of bilateral agreements.

Only after these issues have been extensively discussed without reference to normalization of U.S.-PRC relations are perceptions on either side likely to change. Furthermore, bilateral agreements resulting from these discussions may open up areas for potential negotiations. The flow of goods and people between the two countries can be expanded only through single-issue discussions and the avoidance of complex package agreements that are fraught with risky consequences. Within such a process a time will eventually come when both sides can agree that normalization of relations has in fact been achieved. The announcement of the settlement can be written to convey the same message as the Shanghai Communiqué, namely: both countries recognize that there is only one China, and the government of the United States recognizes that the People's Republic of China is the sole, legitimate government representing the Chinese people residing in the territories it presently controls. This would be in accordance with both historical and current realities. Such a declaration, following the gradual expansion of trade and communications between the two sides, will appear anticlimactic, even lacking in drama, but this is as it should be.

---

[17] In fact, on March 31 a Peking official was quoted as asserting that secret contacts between Taiwan and the Soviet Union were taking place in Vienna. See Paul Hoffman, "Taiwan and Russia Said to Hold Talks," the *New York Times*, April 1, 1978. Taipei denied the report. Whether or not it was true, Peking is concerned about such prospects.

5 ramon h. myers

conclusion

Although the Shanghai Communiqué of February 1972 signalled a new era in the passage of goods and people to and from East Asia, American experts and policy makers alike are still debating the best way to establish full-scale diplomatic relations between the United States and the PRC.

The costs and benefits to the United States of immediate normalization of relations on Peking's terms or gradual issue-by-issue negotiation can be listed and compared, but statistics are neither a convincing nor a sensible basis for charting American foreign policy in East Asia. Foreign policy should be based upon general principles or strategies that are derived from an understanding of the ways states interact in the world. Both the Soviet Union and the PRC act from such a broad perspective; despite their fundamental differences, they both regard the United States and its Western European allies as powerful adversaries to be isolated and weakened whenever possible.

The three policy courses outlined at the outset of this study are based on different ideas about the way the United States should relate to the states of East Asia. One such idea—that of a world dominated by two superpowers, the United States and the USSR, locked in a protracted struggle with each other —forms the basis for a policy of immediate normalization of our relations with the PRC on Peking's terms as a means of opposing the USSR. The belief that no single power can ever dominate the globe sufficiently to influence adversely

American interests and security underlies a second policy—total U.S. withdrawal from East Asia. A third alternative, an American commitment to maintain a stable balance of power among states in East Asia and elsewhere, arises from the perception that checks and balances are required to deter aggressive acts by other states in a world where order is constantly threatened by competition between diverse power groups.

These policies are mutually exclusive: the United States can only choose one. A concession to Peking's terms for normalization of relations would open the door to new pressures for a much closer relationship, even military treaties and an alliance, between the PRC and the United States, but does the belief in a bipolar distribution of power in the world, which underlies this policy, still make sense?

Both the United States and the Soviet Union have serious domestic problems: inflation, unemployment, and growing disillusionment with the conduct of public officials in the former and prospects of declining economic growth and increasing criticism of single-party rule in the latter. Both countries are also deeply involved in new spheres of global interest in the Near East and Africa that require the expenditure of enormous resources and the exercise of considerable diplomatic skills; paradoxically, direct confrontation has been avoided because of these new concerns in far-flung lands. Finally, new centers of power are emerging in the world, for example, in East Asia, and old power centers, such as Western Europe, should not be ignored. The United States and the Soviet Union must now contend with domestic concerns and new international issues that reduce the prospects for confrontation.

A policy of isolation that would lead to total American withdrawal from East Asia is desired neither at home nor abroad. This leaves the United States only one policy option—that of adopting and trying to implement the "equilibrium strategy."

This strategy calls for a moratorium on all discussions related to normalization except by the liaison offices in Peking and Washington, and an avoidance of package-agreement diplomacy, which involves a series of concessions by either one or both sides and great uncertainty for third parties.

What issues can Peking and Washington discuss through their liaison offices? The new leadership in the PRC has recently committed itself to modernizing its economy and its military and educational systems. The potential for rapid economic growth is great provided that regime can obtain the modern technology and capital to improve its industries, infrastructure, and military organizations. In other words, the prospects for trade between the United States and the PRC have never been brighter than they are now, particularly

since the PRC has already achieved a high stage of economic development and is ready to benefit from modern technology.

Trade between the United States and the PRC has declined in the last two years, mostly because of economic setbacks in the latter. Why did the PRC and Japan conclude a U.S. $20 billion eight-year trade pact in early 1978 if the economy of the PRC was in the doldrums? The answer is that Japan's ability to provide a particular package of technology and capital investment that were urgently needed by the PRC made the arrangement possible.

So far there is little evidence that the United States has vigorously tried to divorce trade from politics and negotiate issues separately to achieve similar kinds of agreements. To be sure, the United States has no large semi-official organizations like Japan's Ministry of International Trade and Industry (MITI) that are capable of initiating such discussions with the PRC. Similar arrangements could be worked out, however, if the United States were to adopt a definite policy of preserving the present balance between the two China regimes while undertaking specific bilateral discussions with the PRC.

The "equilibrium strategy" calls for the United States to meet its long-term commitments in East Asia by maintaining existing power relations there. This means pursuing a course of gradualism, avoiding precipitous actions that are likely to leave third parties confused and fearful, and maintaining various military and economic relations that have evolved in the past. This strategy requires a diplomatic style of patient, prudent negotiations on single issues. Although such a style conveys no firm policy course, the underlying idea is always visible.

The equilibrium strategy will eventually produce the following results. If the states that consider the costs of aggression too high can guarantee peace and stability, there will be many new exchanges of goods and people. These exchanges will take place within an interlocking network of separate bilateral agreements. Each side will then begin to see that the flow of benefits from these agreements are too great to lose if any single agreement is broken, and since these agreements depend upon peace and stability, nations will recognize the advantage of maintaining the balance of power in various regions of the world.

It is fitting for this policy study to end with the following caveat. In the last two years the PRC has undergone a tremendous political crisis, and from all appearances has survived it. The transfer of power to new leaders in a totalitarian state is always agonizing and dangerous for domestic stability; the new leadership still must concentrate upon consolidating power and legitimizing its rule. The Chinese Communist Party has been severely demoralized in recent years. This state of nearly one billion people contains administrative provinces

that are equivalent to large European countries; either singly or in combination these provinces might be induced to establish separate rule. In such a critical transition period, the new leadership finds it natural and useful to rally dissident factions and gain popular support for itself through reminders of external threats or concerns, such as Soviet intrusion into China's northern borders or the necessity to liberate Taiwan. Peking's shrill demands for American concessions before normalization of relations can be achieved between the two governments should be judged in this context: they should not be permitted to affect the conduct of U.S. affairs in East Asia. American intransigence on this score merely allows Peking's leaders to continue to use the 'external-issue' tactic to mobilize their country.

index

contributors

RAMON H. MYERS received his Ph.D. in economics from the University of Washington. He was a research fellow at the School of Pacific Studies (department of economics) of the Australian National University between 1965 and 1967, and served as research associate at Harvard University's East Asian Research Center, 1967–1968. He became professor of economics at the Center for Advanced International Studies and the department of economics of the University of Miami in 1967. Since 1975 he has been curator-scholar and research coordinator in the East Asian Collection at the Hoover Institution on War, Revolution and Peace.

WILLIAM W. WHITSON is a graduate of the United States Military Academy and holds a Ph.D. from the Fletcher School of Law and Diplomacy. After a career in the United States Army culminating in the Office of the Secretary of Defense as a member of the Policy Planning Staff, he became a senior social scientist with the Rand Corporation. Later he organized the Directorate of Policy Research at the BDM Corporation before joining the Congressional Research Service as chief of the Foreign Affairs and National Defense Division.

C. MARTIN WILBUR taught modern Chinese history at Columbia University for twenty-nine years before his retirement in 1976. He was a founding member of the East Asian Institute there and its director for six years. He has studied and worked in Shanghai, Peking, and Kunming; he served in the O.S.S. during the Second World War; and he has visited Taiwan eight times, most recently in the summer of 1977. The author of numerous articles and several books on Chinese history, he recently published *Sun Yat-sen: Frustrated Patriot* (Columbia University Press, 1976). He is now George Sansom Professor Emeritus of History at Columbia.

ROBERT A. SCALAPINO received his B.A. from Santa Barbara College, his M.A. and Ph.D. degrees from Harvard University. Since 1949 he has taught in the political science department at the University of California, Berkeley, and has served as chairman for a regular term between 1962–1965, and as interim chairman in 1975. Professor Scalapino has written some 90 articles and more than 10 books or monographs on Asian politics and U.S.-Asian policy. His most recent works include: *Communism in Korea*, 2 vols. (with Chong–Sik Lee), 1972, which received the Woodrow Wilson Award; *Asia and the Road Ahead*, 1975; and *Foreign Policy of Modern Japan* (editor and contributor), 1977. He has traveled extensively in Asia, the Middle East, and Africa, and also spent one month in the People's Republic of China in December–January 1972–1973. Professor Scalapino is a fellow of the American Academy of Arts and Sciences and has served as consultant to many civic groups, foundations, and governmental agencies.

NORMA SCHRODER is a researcher at the National Bureau of Economics–West, investigating the macro-policy implications of household behavior in less-developed countries. She received her B.A and M.A. from the University of Miami (Coral Gables, Florida) and is a doctoral candidate in economics at Stanford University. She has published articles on Chinese agriculture and Taiwan's foreign trade and economic development in *Issues and Studies* (1974) and *International Trade Law Journal* (1976).